STARTING A CRAFT BUSINESS

The Indispensable Guide to Starting a Business for the Creative Artisan

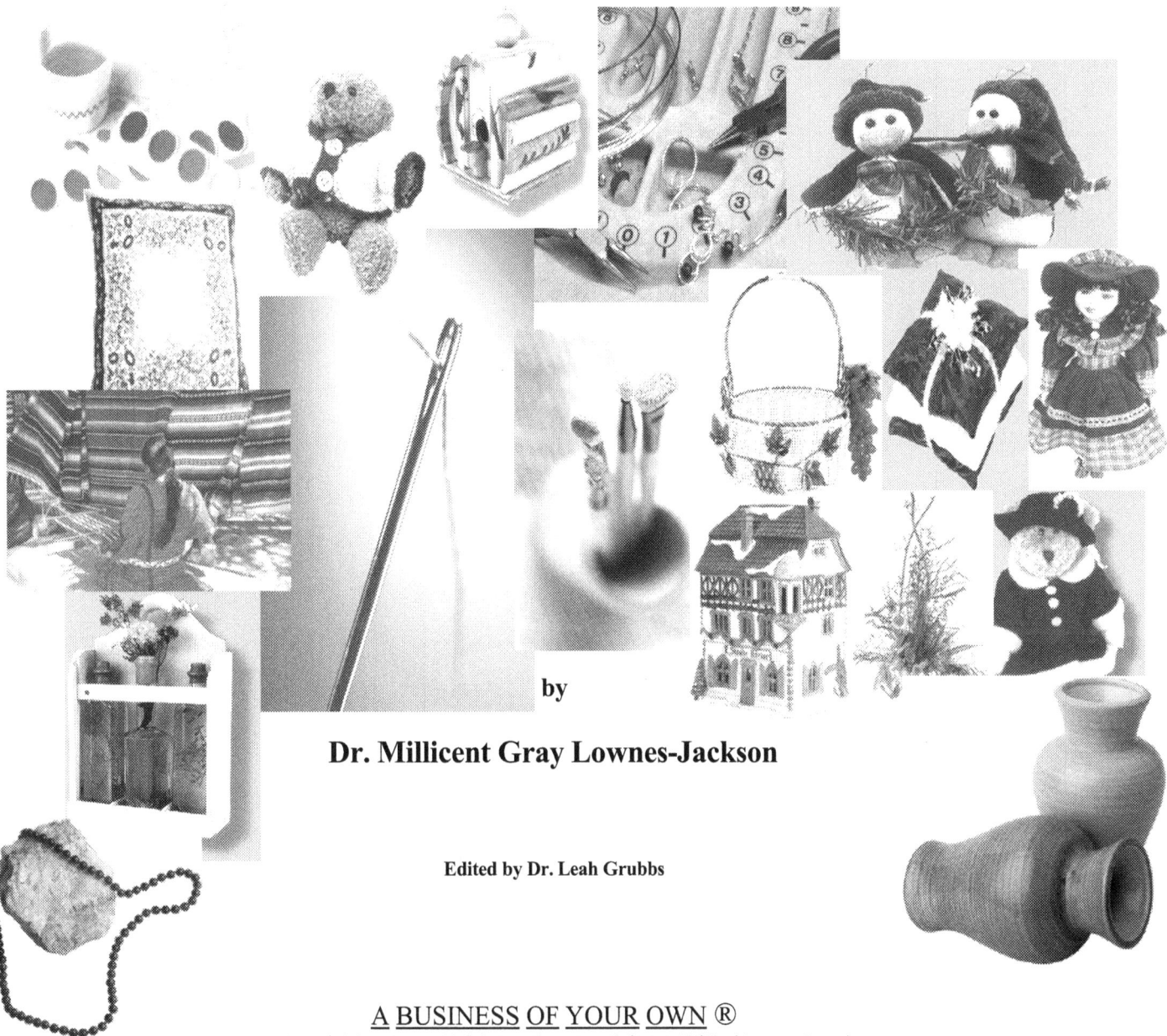

by

Dr. Millicent Gray Lownes-Jackson

Edited by Dr. Leah Grubbs

A BUSINESS OF YOUR OWN ®

BUSINESS PUBLICATIONS AND SERVICES FOR WOMEN

www.ABusinessOfYourOwn.com

Cover designed by Design Visualizations
www. DesignVisualizations.com

CONGRATULATIONS!!!

By merely opening this publication you have taken the first step toward self-fulfilment, financial independence, and taking control of your life. You obviously have an interest in small business ownership and desire to take the informative approach to starting your own business. Effective application of the information presented in this publication will enable you to fulfill your dream of business ownership and financial success. This publication will take you step-by-step through the process of business formulation. At the end of your reading, you will have produced a business plan for your dream and will have identified the specific steps you need to take for implementing your business to be competitive.

A BUSINESS OF YOUR OWN is here to help you pull together the intricate components necessary to make your small business a success. We offer various support services as well as numerous business publications to assist you in pursuit of your entrepreneurial dreams.

We invite you to take the entrepreneurial challenge and wish you much success!

www.ABusinessofYourOwn.com
Mailing address: P.O.B. 210662, Nashville, Tennessee, 37221-0662 (615) 646-3708

OUR SYMBOL   **A ROSE OF PURPLE**

A BUSINESS OF YOUR OWN will help you till the soil and prepare fertile ground for the growth and development of a strong and successful business venture. It will take time. It will take shrewd business savvy. It will take planning and re-planning, and it will take an honest assessment of yourself.

Rose gardens don't just happen overnight. A rose, purple in color, demands very special attention and a great amount of time for development and much nurturing. But, there are few flowers more special than a beautiful, unique rose. The cultivation of a beautiful purple rose is representative of the development of your successful business venture.

The purple rose is distinctive and different. It represents newness, freshness, femininity, and taking the challenge to be different.

Women have intrinsic characteristics that, like a purple rose, can be cultivated. These characteristics can be channeled into a viable avenue of financial independence. But, a woman does not have to lose her uniqueness of being a woman.

A rose of purple, just like a business, requires much time, attention, dedication, knowledge, and nurturing. **A BUSINESS OF YOUR OWN** is here to help you in developing your unique rose.

Our goals are to help cultivate your abilities, assist you in channeling your attributes successfully into a business of your own, encourage you to be the best you can be, provide information to help make you successful in the business world, and at the same time encourage you to maintain your identity and femininity.

A Business of Your Own
BUSINESS PUBLICATIONS & SERVICES
  FOR WOMEN
P.O.B. 210662
Nashville, Tennessee 37221-0662
www.ABusinessOfYourOwn.com
E-*mail:* Success@womaninbiz.com

INFORMATION ABOUT THIS PUBLICATION

The entrepreneurial informational publications of A BUSINESS OF YOUR OWN reflect an enormous amount of in-depth research and the expertise of many noted professionals. In addition to keeping abreast of industry and environmental changes along with new business management techniques and concepts, our staff compiles and presents this information in a readily applicable, easy-to-understand format. Obtaining detailed industry information as presented in our publications would have taken your complete business venture concentration for many, many months. In addition, by purchasing our publications you will avoid the costs that would have been incurred in consulting many professionals and the stress encountered in determining business development procedures.

All information contained in this publication will need to be applied to your particular operating environment, as each environment is unique and exciting. We, therefore, cannot accept responsibility for your success; but we truly believe that the information and the step-by-step approach utilized in this publication will assist you in making more intelligent decisions about the initiation and development of your business.

Even though all companies, resources, and organizations mentioned in this book are believed to be reputable, A BUSINESS OF YOUR OWN cannot accept responsibility for the activities of these parties, nor is A BUSINESS OF YOUR OWN attempting to promote their business efforts.

Congratulations on taking the first step to business success by obtaining the necessary knowledge to realize your dreams.

"There is no fast, challenge-free, road to success.

You have to take it one step at a time and overcome

one challenge at a time and then turn the challenges into

opportunities."

M.G.L.J.

TABLE OF CONTENTS

CHAPTER I

INTRODUCTION

"Success comes to women who

have the courage to dream

and the fortitude to follow their hearts,

coupled with savvy business knowledge and determination."

M.G.L.J.

INTRODUCTION

The quest for business ownership is still very much a part of the American dream, and the entrepreneurial spirit is alive and strong for women. Offering for many, a feeling of personal worth, wealth, prestige, and a way of controlling one's own time and destiny, female-owned businesses represent the fastest growing business sector of the economy. The most recent private research available conducted by the Center for Women's Business Research reports that, as of 2002, there were an estimated 10.1 million majority-owned, privately held 50 percent or more women-owned firms in the United States, employing 18.2 million people and generating $2.32 trillion in sales. Of this 10.1 million, 6.2 million are majority (51%) or more women-owned, and 3.9 million are 50 percent women-owned firms. As of 2002, there were an estimated 1.2 million firms owned by a woman or women of color- amounting to 1 in 5 women-owned firms (20%) in the U.S. Overall, the number of minority women-owned firms increased by 32 percent between 1997 and 2002--four times faster than all U.S. firms and over twice the rate of all women-owned firms. Between 1997 and 2002, the Center estimates that the number of privately held 50 percent or more women-owned firms increased by 11 percent nationwide, nearly twice the rate of all firms; employment increased by 18 percent, and sales grew by 32 percent. [1]

Census Department data uses different definitions for women-owned businesses, requiring that the business be 51 percent owned by a woman before it is classified as woman owned. Thus, Census data reports a fewer number of women-owned businesses, but the bottom line is that women-owned businesses are playing a vital role in the U.S. economy. Women-owned businesses are growing more rapidly than the overall economy and are major contributors to the nation's economic health and competitiveness. Many of these women-owned firms are considered to be micro-enterprises. Generally, these businesses are characterized as having fewer than five employees, a net worth of less than $25,000, and a credit need of less than $15,000. Many of the business owners are women who are underemployed or have low incomes.

National research recently conducted by this writer utilizing survey research methodology provides additional insight into practical entrepreneurial knowledge. Surveys were disseminated via a national business publication as well as a local community newspaper. The survey was designed to ascertain pressing concerns, problems, and stressors experienced by female business owners. A summarization of the findings indicates the following areas of concern as identified by female micro-enterprise owners: organizational ability, selling skills, finding and keeping good employees, managing stress, inequities due to race or sex, inability to obtain government and corporate accounts, inability to break the "ole boy" network, inability to obtain sufficient capital, inability to effectively and efficiently manage operating expenses, feeling isolated, managing time, and the challenge of accepting all responsibility. The issues and concerns raised by this survey population of 200 female micro-enterprise owners reflect the views of those who have taken the entrepreneurial plunge and have provided a sound academic and practical base for compiling the relevant and valuable information contained in this publication.

INDUSTRY OVERVIEW

So, you have extraordinary creative talents. Well, why not enjoy the thrill, exhilaration, and financial rewards of entrepreneurship while enjoying your craft or artistic talent? Why not start a business of your own?

Maybe you simply enjoy making craft items for your friends and family members who love your unique handcrafted works of art. Or, maybe you are selling your art or craft items but want to get organized as a business. Whether your craft is quilting, floral arranging, candle making, ceramics, beading, woodworking, needlecraft, stenciling, wire crafting, exquisite 14K gold jewelry crafting, or any of the myriad of other craft possibilities or art media, you can be a crafty entrepreneur and join the $14 billion crafts industry (The Crafts Report May 2002).[2] As we proceed in the 21st Century with all of its foreseen technological advances, the role of craft businesses remains quite simple. The owner desires to sell various types of handcrafted items or works of art with a goal of making a profit.

Many artisans view themselves more as artists than craftspersons. Interest in art has also intensified greatly in recent years. Individuals from all walks of life are collecting fine art to enliven their homes, to evoke an aura of class, and to invest their money. Many are even shopping for art as a form of entertainment, as a hobby, or as a pastime. Regardless of the reason for collecting art, it is an investment; and when starting an art business, it is important to realize that you are dealing not just with customers but also with investors.

In order to be a successful business owner, awareness of environmental changes and their possible impact on business is a must. The demographics of America are changing. There are more middle-aged adults, career couples, single parents, and blended families with stepchildren, stepparents, and multiple sets of grandparents. The 65-and-over group is growing and becoming more healthy and more active. The country is becoming more diverse, with a higher proportion of blacks, Hispanics, and Asians. Additionally, modern technology has significantly impacted the lives of all Americans. Surprisingly, even though we are in the age of high technology, there has been a great resurgence of interest in the arts and crafts. Many, many Americans have become tired of commonplace, mass-produced items. At the same time, we are looking at a growing market of prosperous young professionals. These new professionals, in many instances, are no longer living near their families but have relocated to a place where their careers can be more promising. These individuals often suffer from nostalgia and long for items that remind them of home and things that "mother used to make." Handmade products of natural materials are in great demand, particularly by "yuppies" who view fine crafts as affordable and desirable art.

Quality merchandise of original design is in demand not only by the public but also by craft shops, galleries, boutiques, flower shops, gift shops, and department stores. The market for craft items and works of art is strong and growing!

The craftsperson or artisan will need to thoroughly evaluate her craft items for marketing potential. What are the aesthetic and physical characteristics of your product(s)? Are your items functional? Do they possess unique characteristics that would appeal to customers? What would make your crafts or art desirable? Who is likely to buy your products (tourists, "baby boomers," senior citizens, wealthy individuals, etc.)? Are similar items being mass-produced which are much cheaper? Why will people demand or desire your art or craft? Where are the majority of your potential buyers located?

LOCATION

When assessing an appropriate location for your business, you need to evaluate not only where your customers are, but also industry trends, what your competition is doing, zoning, growth plans, and your goals and objectives, just to mention a few considerations.

Individuals who decide to sell their craft and art items have the option of having their operations based in their home or operating their businesses from facilities outside of the home. Most craft and art businesses begin as a result of the owner's hobby or hobbies. Therefore, most such businesses begin operations from the home. Home-based businesses are one of the fastest growing segments of the small business sector. An old-fashioned way of conducting business, home-based ventures are presently experiencing a very strong revival which has been advanced by modern technology. With women taking an increased interest in business ownership, a great number have initially elected to start ventures from their homes.

The Home-Based Craft or Art Business

Home-based businesses seem to be attractive to all types of women, be they homemakers, professionals, retirees, divorcees, young singles, or disabled individuals. Many are looking for second incomes; others are using their businesses as their main means of livelihood. Whatever your present situation, examining the operation of your craft business from your home may be a viable and potentially lucrative option.

Why have so many women elected to live and work in the same place? The reasons and attractive features are many.

Advantages of Operating a Home Based Business

Convenience and **reduction of commuting time** to a job outside the home are major advantages. Commuting time is not only a consideration here, but also the elimination of the frustrations experienced in rush hour traffic, the risk of accidents, the wear and tear on your vehicle, car maintenance, and gasoline costs or transit costs are practical elements.

The home-based business owner also has more **control of work hours** than an 8 - 5 worker. If your adrenaline is flowing at 2 a.m., you can work then if you care to do so. You have 24-hour access to your work, your records, your equipment, supplies, etc. As a small business owner, you work for yourself. You can make and break the rules. You **set your own work hours**, determine your own vacation time, and design your unique work environment, you are in control, you are in charge, and your success is totally related to you.

Operating a home-based business allows you to devote time to your **family** when they need you. If you have children, you can even attend your child's school play during the day or have lunch with your husband, children, or friends without worrying about requesting leave time. You can reduce rising child-care costs. You also do not have to lose time on the job because a child has a minor childhood illness. However, a word of caution is in order here. If you find that you cannot operate your business effectively with children underfoot and/or you see that they, along with your work responsibilities, are making you frustrated, you may need to either do most of your work when they are napping or asleep at night, use a "mother's day out" program several days a week, or resort to full-time child care. You cannot be everything to everybody all of the time!

Starting a business from your home allows you to **eliminate normal leasing costs or facility costs** that other small businesses experience. Your utility costs are also lower, and you probably will not need to invest too much in office furnishings. Renovation and redecorating costs are minimized along with modest equipment costs. Working out of the home, in essence, may in many instances give you the competitive edge in the marketplace. You can offer your products or services at a better price than competitors who have high overhead costs. There are also many tax deductions related to your home expenses that can be taken if a portion of your home is designated for business use. You should consult an accountant to make sure you are keeping all of the appropriate records so that you will be in a position to take all legal deductions with appropriate documentation.

Other advantages of operating out of the home include...

- ➤ Financial Benefits
- ➤ Being Able To Take Pride In Running A Successful Business
- ➤ Being Able To Set Your Own Hours And Vacations
- ➤ Being Able To Be Innovative And Creative And Explore New Horizons
- ➤ Elimination Of Office Politics And Problems With Co-Workers
- ➤ Job Enrichment

All of these advantages sound almost too good to believe, but they are accurate and can bring you much success as a crafty or artistic entrepreneur. We do, however, need to assess the disadvantages of working and living in the same place.

Disadvantages of Operating a Home Based Business

When operating a one-person, home-based business, you may experience feelings of **loneliness and isolation**. You don't have people with whom to toss ideas around or to give you creative inspiration, and at times you may question if you're doing things right. Also, you may experience basic periods of depression. You may find that if you do not reach out and remain active in the business community, you get out of the mainstream and feel as if you're always on the outside looking in with your fingers off the pulse of business activity in your community. Overcome the problem of isolation by being active in community organizations that will keep you apprised of community happenings and development plans for your area. This community participation also keeps you and your business visible.

The home-based business owner must have the utmost degree of self-control because a myriad of **temptations** can pull you away from your business focus. Since you determine what to do and when to do it, it is very easy to procrastinate. It is important, therefore, to establish specific work hours. Keep a log of the hours you spend working each day. This will not only tell you if you are cheating yourself but also it will allow you to assess your actual product costs and to determine whether all of the hours you are putting in are worth your while.

Family and friends can be a major area of stress when you attempt to impress upon them that you are working. Quite often if you operate a business from your home, or even from a formalized home studio, your family and friends will not view your business as being as serious as if you were working in a large corporate office. They, therefore, won't mind stopping in to chit-chat or to request your assistance with their problems or concerns, and they certainly won't hesitate to call you on the phone. Try to determine tactful ways of dealing with them, such as, "I really want to talk or meet with you, but I'm in the middle of a project. May I get back with you in a little while?"

Many women working from the home get caught up in the routine of performing **household duties**. Schedule your household work during non-business hours. If you are very organized or if family responsibilities require it, you can throw clothes in the washer and dishes in the dishwasher in the morning; and when you take your morning break, move clothes to the dryer and put dishes up, etc. This will require a great amount of time management skill, but it's a natural to most of us.

When considering the implementation of a home-based business, **zoning** is really the first area that should be addressed. Each community has its own unique zoning restrictions, so check with your local zoning board for the regulations for your area. You don't want to get deeply involved in the process of starting a business that you plan to operate from your home, only to find out that it is not permissible in your area.

Subcultures, politics, and your rapport with your neighbors are also considerations. Even though by law you may be able to operate out of the home, if for some reason your neighbors are jealous of you, or are vehemently opposed to your having a business, they can cause unbelievable problems which could make your step into entrepreneurship a nightmare.

Home-based businesses experience serious problems of **being recognized as a full-fledged business** and must, therefore, put forth special efforts in the areas of image building, reliability, dependability, and quality of products and services. Special attention needs to be given to advertising that focuses on these elements and at the same time attracts attention to your business.

Advertising is particularly important for home-based businesses since most of such businesses are not on heavily traveled thoroughfares and, therefore, cannot rely on walk-in customers or clients. But when advertising your business, you must be careful not to sacrifice your privacy.

Have separate personal and business phones. Use a post office box or suite number as your business address. Pick up and deliver to your customers or clients, if possible, and try to meet with them in their places of business or their homes. All of these suggestions are given not to imply that home-based businesses lack credibility, but to identify sound approaches to separating personal and professional aspects of your daily life. In fact, some businesses are much more attractive to customers if they operate out of the home because customers feel closer to the owner, think they are getting a better buy, are likely to buy more, and feel that they are getting personal attention and special service. For example, customers who know what they want feel better buying directly from an artist or an individual who makes custom-made headboards and bedspreads rather than going through an interior designer. The customers believe they are saving money and may go ahead and get chairs and draperies covered as well.

TO ESTABLISH YOUR BUSINESS'S REPUTATION:

➢ Produce what you promise, when you promise it.

➢ Pay creditors on time.

➢ Produce or offer good quality products and services.

➢ Give customers and clients a "warm and fuzzy" feeling.

In considering the advantages and disadvantages of operating a home-based business, you will need to assess objectively whether living and working in the same place is right for you.

THINK ABOUT IT.....

- How will your family react?

- What will neighbors think?

- With the nature of the business you are considering, will you project the right image and professionalism necessary for success?

- Are home-based businesses allowed in your neighborhood?

- What restrictions and regulations regarding operation of a business from the home exist in your community?

- What insurance will you need for your business including product liability, worker compensation (if you have employees), general liability, fire, theft, etc.?

- Will adjustments be required in your living arrangements, and if so, what costs will be incurred?

- Are you self-disciplined enough to keep the television off while working and to limit personal calls and visits?

- Will you be able to attract quality employees if they are needed?

- Is parking adequate?

- What are your competitors doing? Are they operating from the home or do they have outside business facilities?

Evaluate the pros and cons of starting a business from your home. We have started the list for you with some general advantages and disadvantages. Add all of the advantages and disadvantages that relate to your personal situation, and delete those that are not applicable. Only you can determine whether working and living at the same location will work for you.

PROS	**CONS**
LOWER START-UP COSTS	ZONING CONCERNS & LIMITATIONS
TAX BENEFITS	HOUSEHOLD CHANGES
LIFESTYLE ADAPTABILITY	ESTABLISHING BUSINESS CREDIBILITY
NO COMMUTING HASSLES OR COSTS	LIMITED SPACE
LOWER FIXED COSTS	INTERFERENCE FROM FAMILY & FRIENDS
	DIFFICULTY IN OBTAINING OUTSIDE FUNDING

Locating Outside the Home

Locating your craft or art business outside of the home is a viable option for many. Most craft and art retailers opting to locate outside the home need to consider locating in heavy-traffic areas where there are a great number of potential buyers. Many cities are revitalizing downtown areas which could be a feasible move for a craft or art business. However, the nature and intensity of the customer base will need to be assessed thoroughly. Other sites to consider would be suburban malls and resort sites. However, realize that resort sites are seasonal, and your money will have to be made during the peak period. Craft and art businesses with a unique product and an established clientele have more expansive location options if you're sure your customer base will seek you out.

Of course, you are not limited to your physical location. Mail order catalogs, and the Internet along with placing merchandise strategically in appropriate locations (such as museum shops or hospital gift shops) on a consignment basis could allow you to expand sales significantly from your primary location.

Many craftspeople and artisans are obtaining multiple locations and expanding their products' exposure by using the cart concept. We're not talking about shopping carts, but semi-stationary push carts. These carts, generally fabricated from wood, about 20 feet by 20 feet in size, are positioned on two large wagon wheels. They are commonly colorful with an umbrella or canopy displaying the business name. Pushcarts may be elaborately designed and decorated or very simple, with cost varying accordingly.

Many shopping malls are utilizing the cart concept allowing the mall to be able to offer creative, unique items which small business people want to get to the market. At the same time, the small business owner has a chance to obtain a prime location in a mall at a cost much lower than retail space. Carts also prove to be very lucrative at art festivals, craft shows, airports, hotel lobbies, and just about any place you can find browsers with money to spend. Using the cart concept additionally allows the craftsperson to locate her business at different locations during the week, based on customer volume. For example, one successful craftsperson in Washington, D.C., locates her business five days a week in the renovated post office which has been made into a specialty shopping center and mini-showplace. This allows her to capture the working and tourist crowd during the week. On the weekends, she locates at an upscale shopping center to catch weekend shoppers. Thus, she is able to capture different markets and maximize exposure.

Operating a pushcart, however, requires many long, exhausting hours of work. At the same time, the pushcart operator must have an outgoing personality, along with items unique enough to attract attention. Pushcarts seem to be a more feasible route for individuals selling inexpensively priced items that are unique rather than offering high-priced items.

Using a pushcart may also be an excellent idea for test marketing craft or art items that you are considering marketing via mail order or the Internet. You could lease a cart on a short-term basis and see if your items will really sell before you lay out a lot of cash for Web page development or produce a mail order catalog. Some malls will even let you lease a cart on a weekly basis.

Kiosks can also be found in many malls. Kiosks are stationary little gazebo-like facilities and offer advantages similar to carts, but of course, are not mobile. They may also offer the advantage of creating the feeling the business is more permanent than a movable cart.

One can operate an art or craft business out of one's home and obtain primary exposure of one's artwork on weekends by participating in art shows. Art and craft shows occur all the time across the country. It is up to the business owner to determine if she wants to focus on a particular region or travel nationwide to participate in shows. These shows occur in shopping malls, at fairgrounds, at convention centers, etc. Realize there are costs associated with participating in shows. Time for travelling, the hassles of setting up, and the possibility of losing artwork due to breakage or theft all have to be evaluated. The show format is particularly popular with individuals just starting into an art or craft business as a side business while still maintaining full-time employment. Show levels vary. Some are for the person who wants to be amused while others are more serious. You will need to select strategically the shows in which to participate, based on your type of art and your target market.

Galleries also serve as a location for selling and exposing appropriate art or craft items to the market. Galleries take work either on a consignment basis or buy it outright. Selling your art or craft by consignment constitutes the gallery's accepting your items for inclusion in their collection of offerings. When your items sell, the gallery takes a commission and sends you a check for the remainder. The gallery channel of distribution is frequently used by renowned craftspeople and artisans who don't want to market their products themselves.

Incubation Centers also offer a supportive environment for some art and craft businesses to develop and flourish. Incubation Centers provide rental space for entrepreneurs which is usually offered below the going market rate. They also provide support services which generally include onsite business consultation and centralized business services. In general, they provide a warm, nurturing, and supportive business environment for your business to incubate. Each Incubation Center has its own selection criteria which may exclude certain types of art and craft businesses.

You can be as creative with selecting a location for your business as you are with designing your art or craft items. And, think outside of the box, location doesn't have to be an either/or decision. A major factor to consider, however, is that a location allows you access to as many of your targeted customers as possible at a cost that's feasible and still allows you to make a profit.

Having A Virtual Location

The World Wide Web offers an additional location option, a virtual mall location. Whether you are growing the local or national market for your business or already exploring and pursuing international markets, you need to consider the value of establishing your business presence on the fastest growing marketing medium--the World Wide Web (WWW). In addition to establishing your presence and enhancing your image in the market alongside your competition, the Internet allows your firm to reach a large mass market of educated consumers, 24 hours a day, 7 days a week, year round. A Web presence, however, will not make financial miracles happen or make you a millionaire overnight.

Successful marketing on the Web involves a multi-layered, interactive approach that keeps visitors interested. It should make visitors to your virtual business home feel involved and make them interested in touring your business. It should entice visitors to buy, and provisions should be made for them to be able to buy directly from your site and/or be able to contact you

26

instantly via e-mail. Your Web site should also enable visitors to get on your mailing list as well as let you know how many potential buyers have visited your site.

If you build a better mousetrap, customers will not beat a path to your Web site! In fact, you have to market your Web site continuously. Your Web address should be included on all of your printed materials (ads, letterhead, cards, brochures, bags, etc). You also have to be aggressive using strategies such as link exchanges, continuously submitting site information to search engines, as well as to print advertising, and having a creative e-mail address which puts your Web name out there every time you give out your e-mail address. An example of a creative e-mail might be Elegance@mycrafts.com.

The Craft Organization Development Association (formerly the Craft Organization Directors Association) (CODA) recently conducted research about Web marketing usage among craftspeople and found that some are making money and some are not.[3] (The Crafts Report January 2001). So the verdict is not in for craft business success on the Web. The study, however, did find that the longer a craftsperson had a Web presence, the greater were the chances of making money via the Web. It was also found that more craft artists are making money from retail sales online than from wholesale sales online.

Ten years ago, a business with a Web Home Page was considered unique and on the "cutting edge," but now, in business circles, it is expected, especially among companies that wish to be thought of as having business savvy. To maximize your use of the numerous technological advances in the area of e-commerce and to determine if a Web site is feasible for your business, you should contact a computer consultant who can assess the actual needs for your particular business and can also design your Web Page or refer you to a Web designer. College campuses are also a good source for students studying e-commerce who may be able to take on your project as a class project at no cost to you.

Many artists are also electing to market their art on-line via auction sites such as e-bay. This marketing strategy is also coupled with a compelling Web site that allows potential buyers to view all of the artisan's available works of art.

Regardless of the nature of the art or craft business, to be prosperous, an art business must have a good location (or combination of locations), a good merchandise mix, sound business methods, and an owner who's willing to work hard to make the business a success.

PRODUCTION

Ideally, the craftsperson should have a separate work area to produce her or his craft. Even if the work area is in the home, it should be a separate work space with room for storage of supplies, finished items, a place for preparing items for display, a place for keeping business records, and room for producing the craft or art with adequate room for equipment.

EQUIPMENT AND SUPPLIES

The actual supplies and equipment required for your craft or art business will, of course, vary based on the nature of your business. When purchasing equipment, make sure you consider projected volume and efficiency requirements. You don't want to invest in equipment, just to find out a couple of months later that you need additional capacity equipment. At the same time, you don't want to "overbuy" in the equipment area, taking up needed funds. In essence, you need to assess thoroughly your market prior to purchasing equipment as well as evaluate your need for supplies and tools.

Many artisans and craftspeople elect to buy used equipment or to lease equipment and tools until they have a clear feeling of the direction in which their business is going. Another option is to buy equipment jointly with other individuals in other crafts. Cooperative or group purchases of materials and equipment is quite popular among artisans and craftspeople. This allows for advantageous volume discounts that otherwise would be unavailable. A word of caution is in order for those electing to co-op with other individuals. Make sure all of the details of the relationship are spelled out in writing, including rights for the use of equipment, when you can use equipment, who pays for repairs, dissolution of the arrangement, who makes the decision to upgrade the equipment, and how revenue from the sale of the equipment will be distributed.

SOURCES OF SUPPLY AND INVENTORY

Before it can be determined that a business is feasible, it is necessary to identify sources from which the entrepreneur may obtain goods, either for use in the business or for resale. The entrepreneur may determine, based on the prices of goods purchased from the supply source and the necessary mark-up in light of overhead, that it will be too difficult to compete on a price basis with competitors.

Craft and art businesses often start off buying supplies from a local retail supplier. When the business grows enough to warrant buying supplies in large quantities, wholesalers or distributors should be evaluated for merchandise. It is important that a business not be developed relying totally on one supplier. If the business encounters problems with this one supplier or the supplier is slow in the delivery of purchases, the entrepreneur's operations may be significantly affected. It is best to use several supply sources continuously so as to establish good credit and rapport with these firms. Resultantly, the entrepreneur will get better service once he or she is recognized as a consistent customer.

It is important to have an inventory control system set up which will indicate when you need to reorder certain items. Inventory records allow one to keep an accurate account of the amount and nature of inventory at any one point. Maintaining inventory records by hand can be a complicated and tedious chore. Using electronic data processing (EDP) can provide the entrepreneur with valuable information allowing time to make good purchasing decisions quickly.

QUALITY CONTROL

Quality control requires mentioning because the reputation of a business rests highly on the standards maintained. Of course, when dealing with handcrafted items or original works of art, no two items will be exactly alike, but pre-determined standards must be kept. If you desire to hire others to assist with production, quality control becomes even more crucial because, generally speaking, no one will be as committed to your business as you are.

DISTRIBUTION

Artisans and craftspeople have several distribution options for selling their merchandise. You can sell directly to the individuals who will use the art or craft item, or sell to stores which in turn sell to the ultimate user of the item, or sell to wholesalers who in turn sell to retailers.

30

Selling to retailers is considered wholesaling. You may wish to approach appropriate retail stores in your area to get them to sell your works of art. Another route to reach more of a national market is to approach buyers of large retail operations. You may also want to approach wholesale firms that sell a wide array of crafts, art, and/or decorative accessories to retailers across the country.

You may elect to market your items yourself or use sales representation or distributors in the industry. Distributors often buy your items outright at a negotiated discount price. The distributors then have their sales staff sell your items with other items from other artists or craftspeople to appropriate stores. You, in essence, receive payment before merchandise is actually sold to retail establishments. Sales representatives, on the other hand, generally operate either on a straight commission or a salary plus commission basis. Monies are received only after sales are made.

Mail order distribution is another method of distribution often selected by craftspeople. Implementing a successful mail order marketing plan will require much research and investigatory work on the part of the business owner. Developing an impressive mail order catalog can also be costly, and appropriate mailing lists of individuals primed to purchase your specific items may be difficult to obtain.

THE PRESENTATION PACKAGE

Regardless of whether you use an agent or conduct the marketing yourself, you will need a presentation package of your work. This could be very elaborate, produced with color photographs or prepared quite simply. The important point is that you need a presentation

31

package when approaching retailers and wholesalers. The presentation package should give an overview of your business and provide information about your items. Pictures of your products, colors available, stock numbers, prices, minimum order sizes, terms of payment, and any available discounts should be included. The presentation package is a major marketing tool for your business and should reflect the image you are trying to project.

OBTAINING EXPOSURE

In addition to obtaining exposure and creating sales by marketing items through wholesale and retail establishments, artists and craftspeople often exhibit at art and craft shows. Shows occur throughout the country at various times of the year. They vary in sophistication, professionalism, size, and market appeal. Many part-time artisans primarily use this method for marketing their items on the weekends.

It is important to select strategically the shows and fairs in which you participate. If the show has a reputation for "cheap" items, and if you are trying to project a quality image with high price tags, you will lessen the perceived value of your products. Start right now by visiting shows and fairs in your area or in parts of the country of interest to you. Research the shows, examining the participants, the quality and types of art and/or crafts, the type of customers visiting the show, and the type of publicity announcing the show. Pay attention to the show or fair sponsors. Start your planning for show participation in the approaching year by evaluating your assessments of the various shows and fairs. Make sure you get your applications in early for your selected shows.

For those who view themselves as artists, exhibits are a way to expose their talents. There are three basic types of exhibits in which the artist may be interested: open-juried exhibits, museum invitational exhibits, and one-artist shows.

Open-Juried Exhibits. Juried exhibits are generally sponsored by art galleries or organizations. Entries are evaluated by a group of experts with the entries viewed as best receiving awards. Exhibits provide an opportunity for the artist to receive exposure, to sell art, and to evaluate how her or his art compares to other artists. However, the artist should realize that participating in exhibits is expensive.

Museum Invitational Exhibits. Artists may participate in invitational exhibits if they are asked to display art by the museum. Artists, however, don't have to wait to be invited. You can request an interview to show your portfolio. If the museum staff is impressed, they will extend an invitation to you to participate in the exhibit.

One -Artist Shows. These shows, as the name indicates, are those with only one artist's work is on display. This is a highly desirable situation, particularly if the show is sponsored by a choice gallery or museum in one of the major art centers.

AGENTS FOR THE ARTIST

Successful merchandising of artwork requires as much skill, talent, and creativity as is required to produce the art. Many artists realize that their forte is in producing masterpieces versus the marketing end of the art. As a result, agents have surfaced in this industry as major role players.

An agent is a businessperson who promotes the work of artists. The agent represents the artist and handles business concerns for the artist who desires to sell her or his artwork. The agents only take on a client if they believe that the time, energy, and money they put into publicizing an artist's work will be beneficial. Therefore, if you have not established a reputation, you will have to sell yourself to an agent.

Utilizing an agent allows the artist to devote all of her or his time to artwork. Agents are helpful if the artist is a part-time art person and works full-time at another job. An agent allows the artist to expand her or his reputation beyond the immediate vicinity and is particularly helpful if the artist is not a salesperson. The agent can also "brag" about the artist's reputation, talent, and accomplishments more comfortably than you could about yourself. Additionally, agents can take care of collecting monies due, arrange showings, and provide assistance with pricing art.

Your time and your ability to afford agent fees are important factors to consider when determining if you need an agent. Having an agent also lends credibility to the value of your art.

THE AGENT AND ARTIST RELATIONSHIP

The monetary relationship between the artist and agent is very simple. The artist provides the agent with artwork for which a receipt is given. When the art is sold, the agent gives the monies, less the agent's commission, and a copy of the bill of sale to the artist. All aspects of the artist/agent relationship should be covered by a written contract.

The artist/agent arrangement should address all potential problems or areas of concern.

Major areas to be covered include:

- ➤ Percentage of selling price to be received by agent.

- ➤ Whether the agent gets a percentage of all sales, including those made by the artist, or just a percentage of sales the agent makes.

- ➤ The exact nature of the promotional activities the agent will engage in for the artist.

- ➤ Whether the agent or the artist establishes the price on art and limits on pricing authority.

- ➤ The time period of the arrangement.

- ➤ Whether more than one agent can be used by the artist.

Some artist/agent relationships involve the agent's buying the artist's work outright. It is best to have an attorney formalize the specifics of your relationship with an agent.

YOU AS AN AGENT

In addition to utilizing agents or dealers, many artists are employing their own marketing strategies and serving as their own agents. Some are featuring limited editions of their artwork. This strategy invites individuals to invest in an entire collection, implies quality and distinctiveness, and at the same time, lowers the price of the artwork so that the market is expanded. In essence, artwork that was formerly limited to the wealthy is obtainable by individuals with less than affluent status who want to invest in art.

Some artists have even worked in mail order selling, and many are establishing their own art galleries or stores in order to market their artwork. Of course, if you sell your own art, you will work more conscientiously than an outsider. If you market your own art, you will also avoid the cost of an agent. Furthermore, you may even get a thrill out of selling your art. However, if you want to work full-time at your artwork or if you primarily do artwork during your spare time while holding down a full-time job, then you may seriously want to consider utilizing the services of an agent. You may also want to consider using an agent if you wish to expand your name recognition and reputation.

SELLING TO MUSEUMS

Most artists view having a museum buy their art as a statement of having "made it." Certainly, there is an implied distinction that makes the sale to a museum desirable. This is particularly the case if the museum is well known and will be instrumental in convincing dealers and collectors to seek your art.

You can sit and wait for a museum to contact you, or you can help the museum become interested in you. This is where strategic marketing comes into play. First, you should identify the museums that focus on your type of art. Then, you should keep them aware of your advancement, sending them news clippings, etc. about exhibits or shows in which you are participating. Develop contacts in the museum and keep in touch. This should be a well planned marketing campaign culminating with the purchase of your art.

OWNING A RETAIL STORE

By selling your own art and/or crafts directly to the final consumer, you avoid intermediaries and are able to maximize your profits. You also maintain control over the manner in which your items are sold and are able to encourage sales by adding important artisan and craft information that could make the consumer appreciate the time and skill that went into producing your items. Realize, however, that when you have your own store, you will have to keep a wide range of items available. This means you will need to keep inventory available, which means more production. But how can you produce more if you now have to direct former production time to managing a business?

Multiple responsibilities and tasks can become difficult, and require the artisan either to hire individuals to help with production or to help with the store. This means the artisan or craftsperson now has become a businessperson and manager versus just an artist.

The owner of a craft or art store needs to be a people-oriented person. She or he should like working with customers and should have the ability to give customers a "warm and fuzzy" feeling when they enter the establishment. If this isn't you, and you had rather stay with the artistic end of the business, you may want to look at hiring someone to manage your store.

You may also elect to augment your craft or art items with those of other artisans or with a line of gift items. This allows you to reduce production levels and, at the same time, widen your market potential. This option must be evaluated in light of the overall production and inventory costs saved. Visiting the permanent showrooms and gift shows held at the regional marts which follow will help you become acquainted with possible wholesalers for your art or craft items, as well as provide resources for gift items you may be interested in carrying. Having a temporary exhibit during one of the regional gift shows will also allow you to maximize your exposure to gift shop buyers. A listing of major gift marts follows.

MAJOR GIFT MARTS

NEW YORK	New York Merchandise Mart 41 Madison Avenue New York, NY 10010 (212) 686-1203 www.41madison.com
DALLAS	Dallas Market Center 2100 Stemmons Freeway Dallas, TX 75207 (214) 655-6100 or 800-DAL-MKTS www.dallasmarketcenter.com
ATLANTA	Atlanta Merchandise Mart AMC, Inc./AMERICASMART®-ATLANTA 240 Peachtree Street, Suite 2200 Atlanta, GA 30303 (404) 220-3000 www.americasmart.com
CHICAGO	The Merchandise Mart, Chicago Chicago, IL 60654 (800) 677-MART www.merchandisemart.com
LOS ANGELES	The L. A. Mart Los Angeles, CA 90007 (800) LAMART.4 www.lamart.com
MIAMI	Miami International Merchandise Mart 777 N.W. 72nd Avenue Miami, FL 33126 (305) 261-2900 www.miamimart.net

Each supplier will need to be examined individually, and some trial and error will have to occur before the new firm can identify the vendors most in tune with the complete personality of its business. Visiting trade shows and merchandise marts will allow you to view merchandise from many vendors and conduct comparative analyses.

Most diversified craft and art stores buy from various suppliers and attempt to diversify merchandise offerings frequently. Shops in heavy tourist areas, however, do not have to be as concerned about offering different varieties of merchandise too frequently since tourists are usually not repeat customers. Of course, it is important to identify the suppliers with whom you feel very comfortable concerning product quality, terms of payment, delivery time, and return policies. Often times, brand recognition on the part of the customer is also an important determinant in selecting vendors.

In addition to the suppliers that may be identified by visiting one of the regional marts just listed, appropriate suppliers or vendors can also be located by examining indexes such as The Thomas Register.

VENDOR TERMS

When buying gift items or antiques to incorporate with your artwork, it is important to be familiar with buying-term possibilities. The terms of wholesalers are very important to cash flow concerns. Buying terms are often directly related to a good credit rating. A good credit rating will allow you to obtain "NET 30" terms, allowing payment within 30 days after invoice date. This, of course, allows you to use your money for that period rather than having to allocate cash when the order is placed.

Some suppliers offer terms such as "2/10" or "1/10," meaning that retailers may take a two percent or one percent discount if the bill is paid within 10 days of the invoice date. Many times suppliers will not tell you of these term possibilities, so do not hesitate to ask. You have nothing to lose.

Other terms to ask about are quantity discounts and freight allowances in which the supplier agrees to pay the freight costs. Freight costs can really add up, ultimately passing the cost on to the customer. Freight costs raise your price per item which could affect your competitive position in the market.

Suppliers generally have minimum orders, but many will allow you to purchase less than the minimum with an additional cost being incurred by you. In some cases, incurring the additional cost may be feasible.

ESTABLISHING CREDIT WITH VENDORS

Establishing credit with vendors is a tough area. When you are new and approach a supplier about trying to establish credit, the supplier will ask you for credit references from other vendors. But how can you have credit references from other suppliers when you are a new business?

You will need to identify suppliers who are willing to work with new firms. It may require a lot of work, research, and face-to-face contact with suppliers at a merchandise mart or trade show for you to identify good suppliers who are willing to work with new firms as they attempt to establish credit.

Buy from the supplier several times and pay with a check. Be able to present a letter of credit worthiness from your banker. This may have to be a letter regarding your personal accounts if your business account has no track record. The company, of course, is going to wait until your check clears the bank before they ship the merchandise. After this is done with several orders, you will have established credit with them, and then that supplier can be used as a reference for other vendors. Clarify on the front end at what point you will be able to establish credit or at what point they will bill you versus requiring cash. Also clarify when they will serve as a reference to other vendors.

STORE DESIGN

It is important for retail establishments, such as art galleries and craft and gift businesses, to stay progressive, not only in merchandise offerings but also in store layout, fixtures, design, atmosphere creation, etc. Periodic visits to merchandise marts and retail establishments in large cities can keep the retailer full of fresh, innovative, and exciting ideas for encouraging sales.

The design of an artistic business is of utmost importance, as it must create an aura that will make individuals want to enter your establishment, browse, and buy. The atmosphere must inspire customers to buy, buy, buy, and feel good about buying from you.

The exterior and interior of the facility must be consistent with the image you have established for your firm, just as everything you do must project the same image.

The exterior should identify your business by some sort of readily visible sign using your business logo. If feasible, the exterior should also consist of display windows which contain craft and/or artwork that captivates in a quick glance and shows the type of merchandise you carry. Color and style are important for exterior design and should incorporate the color motif used in your logo. These elements should also be tied into the business image and flavor which you are attempting to project to the public.

Interior appearance, of course, is important. Store layout is crucial. If customers can

41

simply walk into the center of your gallery, take a quick glance around and easily walk out, your objective of selling has not been accomplished. You will have to decide what is right for you and your environment, considering the space you have available. Some retailers use a flow plan that forces customers to pass all of the merchandise. Some use nooks and crannies to entice customers.

Simple things, such as appropriate lighting conducive to buying and accentuating your artwork, plush carpet, and the type of store fixtures or display tables on which merchandise is placed, can add the inspiration to buy. Interior design and layout must be supplemented with pleasant salespeople, and, perhaps, even complimentary beverages and/or candy to create that "warm and fuzzy" feeling.

PERSONNEL

The small craft and art store generally cannot afford a great number of employees who are specialists or extremely well trained. Therefore, the owner of a small art store will need to hire employees who are adaptable and can perform various tasks. The employees should be able to convey the atmosphere that you want your store to have. They should be thoroughly trained in store procedures, friendly, honest, patient, and knowledgeable of merchandise features. Customers are "turned off" by pushy, abrasive salespeople and sales personnel who are unable to answer the simplest questions about merchandise. Most art and craft businesses hire a small number of employees and rely heavily on part-time assistance. Retired art teachers, art enthusiasts, and art students are good personnel resources. The owner will have to put forth a concerted effort to keep employees motivated and develop a team spirit.

SERVICES

Art and craft establishments frequently offer amenities such as accepting credit cards, gift wrapping, gift certificates, delivery, in-house credit accounts, and even bridal and gift registries. Again, you will need to assess your operating environment to determine which services are appropriate for your business.

SECURITY

Art and craft establishments need to be aware of the theft techniques used by shoplifters and burglars, as well as employees. The provisions the art store owner can take to guard against crime are numerous; and the selection of appropriate preventive measures will be contingent upon the store's operating environment, money available to spend on preventative methods, and insurance requirements.

Preventive measures which can be taken include security mirrors, door and window locks, closed-circuit television systems, guard dogs, silent alarms, bells that ring when customers walk in, security patrols, fake security cameras, locked display cases for expensive items, an effective screening system for job applicants, watching the cash register or cash box, paying attention to inventory levels, and having alert employees, just to mention a few.

PRICING

Pricing is a difficult area. Each craft and art item should pay for the shelf it sits on, and that includes all of the overhead such as electricity, sales personnel, and operating expenses associated with the item. In determining price, therefore, there must be a sufficient mark-up over the actual cost of the item to cover all direct and related costs and to give you a reasonable profit. At the same time, your pricing needs to consider the image you are trying to project and for what price your competition is selling similar merchandise. Also, don't forget to put a value on your time and creative expertise that went into making each item. These values should be factored into the actual cost of producing each item.

If you are positioning your handcrafted work as art, you must price your work so that it is viewed as a valuable investment. At the same time, the purchasers must feel that they have received a value for their monetary outlay. Pricing artwork is very difficult because of the complexity in placing a precise value to art. Many intangibles, such as ability, skill, reputation, and talent, come into play when pricing art on which it is hard to attach a dollar value. How the individuals in the area in which you are selling your art value art and what your style of art is are factors that affect pricing.

A good starting point for pricing art is to look at the minimum you could charge. The base minimum consists of all material costs, supply costs, and basic "out-of-pocket" costs, overhead costs (costs for heat, rent, light, phone, etc. broken down to an hourly overhead rate) and a time charge (found by placing an hourly value on your work and multiplying by the number of hours the art piece took to complete). Most artists find that the majority of the sales are low- and medium-priced pieces.

Some effective strategies for stimulating sales are given in the following list.

SUCCESS STRATEGIES FOR STIMULATING SALES

⇒ Be knowledgeable of art and/or crafts. Know the terms.

⇒ Determine the "tastes" of customers in your area.

⇒ Specialization in certain media is often feasible and allows you to be an expert.

⇒ Art galleries generally have a low volume of sales. Take this into consideration as you consider your overhead and project sales.

⇒ Higher priced art items require more contemplation on the part of the customer, so be patient and courteous to individuals who visit your establishment numerous times before purchasing anything. This also alludes to the fact that you will need to use good sales skills to really make that customer desire the contemplated item. Sometimes tactfully mentioning the fact that they can pay over a period of time will bring about that purchase.

⇒ Many art and craft stores have been successful by incorporating other related merchandise that has a quicker turnover rate than artwork and which encourages the non-normal art purchaser to visit the business.

⇒ Locating in an older building such as an old mansion or in an historic district can create the right atmosphere for purchasing art and handcrafted items.

⇒ Capture the tourist trade if possible.

⇒ Consider using older, knowledgeable salespeople who love art and crafts.

⇒ Starting an art lovers or craft lovers club can encourage sales.

⇒ Holding art and crafts classes can arouse an interest and encourage sales.

⇒ Sponsor tours to art-infested areas of the country.

⇒ Identify businesses with unused space and make a proposal that you place artwork there on consignment (e.g. bookstore or restaurant). This allows you to get additional exposure and promote sales. The business has nothing to lose.

⇒ Encourage REALTORS to buy artwork for their clients as appreciation tokens for purchasing a home through them.

⇒ Don't forget that schools and organizations sponsor silent auctions which will allow you to obtain promotion for the low cost of donating an item from your collection. Make sure the donated item is indicative of the quality of merchandise you carry and speaks positively about your firm, and make sure there is no chance that it will be sold too inexpensively.

⇒ Small door prizes at luncheons and other activities are an inexpensive form of advertising and, at the same time, create goodwill.

⇒ Approach interior designers and let them know what you have to offer and provide them incentives, such as discounts, to buy from you.

⇒ Restaurants and other businesses are often in need of decorative items to beautify their establishments. You can provide them with decorative art in return for their retaining your business identification card on the merchandise while in use. Lamp stores easily lend themselves to utilizing art for accentuation. Flower shops and clothing stores can also use art and crafts creatively. Don't forget the little things such as attractive identification cards with your business information.

⇒ Consider special services, including gift wrapping and delivery service.

⇒ Hold a holiday "Open House" at Easter, Christmas, Hanukkah, Independence Day or other appropriate time

⇒ Provide decorations for fashion shows and other community events either free or at a discount. (Make sure you get publicity from the donation.)

⇒ If you have a store and an extra room, let civic groups use it in the evening for meetings. This creates goodwill and also encourages sales.

⇒ Appear on television talk shows. Also, periodically send craft and art items to television talk shows. They will probably thank you and your business on the air, plus it will give you an entree for future publicity coverage.

⇒ Keep local newspapers informed about your activities that provide any community service such as free demonstrations.

⇒ Play an active role in community groups and civic affairs.

⇒ If you have a store, periodically change your display windows and move inventory around so that frequent customers will see new things every time they visit your establishment.

INDUSTRY SUMMATION

Craftwork represents a hobby for some; but for others, it is an occupation in the field of art resulting from formalized training. Regardless of the background or motive of the craftsperson, there is a great demand for the creative, unique goods provided by craftspeople. It is important for the craftsperson to realize that there is a big difference between making an item and selling an item. The craftsperson must move from the mindset of being an artist to being a businessperson. This can be extremely difficult for individuals who are primarily intrigued by the enjoyment of their craft.

The market for craft items is strong, growing, and holds many opportunities for the progressive artisan who can transfer some of her or his creative abilities to creative marketing with sound business knowledge and who is prepared to take the entrepreneurial challenge.

Prescription for Success

Self Confidence
Unwavering Focus with a Plan
Commitment to Community
Communication Skills
Ethics, Enthusiasm, Energy, Education
Sound Goals and Selling Skills
Spirituality

M.G.L.J.

CHAPTER II

CONSIDERING THE CHALLENGE

THE ENTREPRENEURIAL CHALLENGE

Business ownership is **a challenging, exhilarating, yet exhausting** way of life. The road to business success is filled with **risk, problems, and pitfalls**. The business owner **must meet these frustrations with perseverance**. An attitude of perseverance, in light of future rewards, helps the business owner to continue the commitment to business. **Perseverance, continual planning, and hard work** enable the business owner to overcome the obstacles inherent in any new venture.

Small business ownership can be a reality for you. Identify your passion, turn your passion into a profitable venture through planning, and, above all, persevere to create **a business of your own that fulfills your dreams** for the future.

ON TO THE CHALLENGE....

CONSIDERING THE CHALLENGE

"Like creating the intricate components of a computer system or cultivating a rose garden, pulling together all the elements of a successful small business is an art that requires knowledge, skill, hard work, experience, and much determination." MGLJ

Are you an individualist, an independent type of person, an adventurer? Are you a risk taker? Do you dislike taking common orders and doing the same thing every day? Do you like the freedom of working independently? Do you like testing your own talents and reaping benefits directly from your personal efforts? Do you desire to use your ideas, abilities, ambitions, aspirations, and initiative to the greatest degree? If you answer "yes" to most of these questions, then maybe you need to consider owning "a business of your own."

Are you tired of your present work environment or tired of the routine? Do you feel that you are in a rut? Do you feel that your abilities go overlooked? Maybe you simply desire a chance to make more money. Are you a displaced homemaker needing to find a way to support yourself? Maybe you have just found a new craft hobby or artistic channel, and you know you are exceptional and think you should capitalize on your talent. Maybe your creative spirit is simply restless or, perhaps you just have spare time on your hands, and you never thought before about making money while enjoying a craft or form of art. If any of these examples fit you, then small business ownership may be the answer allowing you to realize many of your dreams.

There is no question that all people are not qualified to be business owners, nor is there any question that persons who wish to establish a business must depend on their own qualifications and abilities to "make it" or "break it." Going into business is a major decision requiring much commitment.

Business-success potential is highly related to the personal attributes of the business owner. Many studies have been conducted regarding the personal requirements necessary for small business success. Certain common characteristics have been found among successful women who have started businesses. Successful entrepreneurs tend to be decisive and versatile. They follow tasks through to completion. They are self-confident. They are persistent. They have knowledge of the fields in which they start their businesses. They have a strong degree of drive. They are creative and analytical thinkers and have good human relations skills.

AM I DESCRIBING YOU?

Women have unique talents and skills, instilled during childhood, which may be reflected in their daily lifestyles and which may be channeled effectively into a business venture. Simple activities normally taken for granted, such as managing the home and managing children, coordinating activities for social organizations, the ability to do 10 things at one time, delegating chores and responsibilities at work or at home, organizing a car pool, keeping the boss organized, or being responsible, reliable, and economical are all talents that frequently go unappreciated and overlooked. They are sometimes even looked down on because they are viewed as being traditional female values or female stereotyping. But, ladies, whether you view yourself as liberated or not, we need to look at ourselves and assess all of these abilities which can easily be transferred into dollars in the business world.

The typical craftsperson or artisan comes from many different walks of life and varied stations of life to the entrepreneurial table. Shirley of Nashville, Tennessee, was an aggressive and outgoing administrator in the field of social work when she became disabled and couldn't maintain a full-time job. Searching for a way to keep her mind active, Shirley moved into the world of crafts by chance, or others may call it divine intervention. She was browsing in the sewing and craft section of her local Wal-Mart in her wheelchair and ran into a church member who asked her what she was getting ready to make. Shirley replied, "I don't know, I can't sew, and I don't knit or crochet; I'm just looking." The church member said, "Well, I'll teach you how to sew." The church member taught Shirley to hand sew in her backyard in the middle of winter and in the snow as Shirley's wheelchair could not fit through her front door. Shirley has mastered sewing, even though she still claims she's a novice. She makes highly demanded lap throws for ladies in wheelchairs along with beautifully laced handkerchiefs, bedspreads, baby quilts, and sheets. Shirley doesn't make a lot of money and says she's not really in business to make money, but more in business to brighten the lives of others, as she loves to make items to give to nursing homes and senior citizens in her church. Shirley's life plan certainly never included a career in the crafts industry, but Shirley has used her God-given talents to map out a way to bring her life meaning and joy while bringing joy to others.

Women should realize that they have many inherent talents and abilities and even general concern for humankind which are often taken for granted and have exceptional transferability to the business world. In fact, according to a recent study conducted by the Craft Organization Directors Association (CODA), the typical craftsperson is a woman, Caucasian, the average age of 49.[4]

All of us have unique abilities and skills. An in-depth, self-evaluation process will allow you to identify your strongest areas and focus on interests and abilities which could be channeled strategically and successfully into a business venture. This process is a necessity prior to starting a business.

Later in this chapter, we proceed with this process and examine your qualities in light of the characteristics common among successful entrepreneurs. But let's first review the research related to entrepreneurial success characteristics.

Individuals contemplating going into business for themselves should be aware of the personal attributes required for success as an entrepreneur. Numerous studies suggest that there are certain personal requirements or personality characteristics which successful small business owner-managers seem to have in common. One such study was conducted by a team of psychologists at Case Western Reserve University. This study utilized tests, questionnaires, and in-depth interviews to examine characteristics of chief executive officers of several successful small businesses. The study resulted in the following profile of the successful entrepreneur:[5]

1. The successful entrepreneur is a moderate risk taker--not a gambler. He [or she] is an adventurer.

2. The successful small business person is decisive and tends to like tight control over decision making.

3. The successful small business person is versatile and tends to strive for competence in many business areas.

4. The successful small business person is a finisher. He [or she] tends to have strong motives to achieve and endure until the completion of a task.

5. The successful small business person is self-confident. He [or she] has a strong belief in his [or her] own capabilities.

6. The successful business person is a benevolent despot, and he [or she] tends to be friendly and willing to listen to the suggestions of subordinates.

Another study of personality characteristics that lead to success in small business was made by H. B. Pickle. He identifies five characteristics he considers significant.[6]

1. Drive--comprised of responsibility, vigor, initiative, persistence, and health;

2. Thinking Ability--comprised of original or creative analytical thinking;

3. Human Relations Ability—comprised of ascendancy, emotional stability, sociability, cautiousness, consideration, cheerfulness, cooperation, and tact;

4. Communications Ability--both oral and written; and

5. Technical Knowledge--comprised of acquired skills developed through study and practical application.

A review of the literature on small business initiation, ownership, and management leads to the conclusion that there are various personal attributes necessary for success in entrepreneurship. The Small Business Administration (SBA), the governmental agency which assists small businesses, identifies certain personal attributes as being necessary for entrepreneurial success. Included in the list are the following 18 characteristics and abilities:

- Understanding of others,

- Willingness to take a chance,

- Ability to withstand stress,

- Ability to take over when the going gets rough,

- Honesty in business relationships,

- Selling skills,

- Spirit to meet competition,

- Ability to keep abreast of new technology in the field, as well as environmental changes,

- Initiative and leadership abilities,

- High capability for organizing,

- Industriousness and capability to work long hours,

- Ability to make and guide accurate decisions,

- Perseverance (not discouraged by obstacles),

- Desire to get ahead with a high level of energy,

- Ability to understand customers and their desires,

- Ability to adapt to change,

- Innovativeness, and

- Ability to inspire and direct or motivate[7]

There has been considerable interest in the nature of the entrepreneur for many years, but interest in the female entrepreneur has surfaced only recently. This interest has been generated by the recognition that the entrepreneur is a central figure in economic activity. However, relatively little research has been done on the female entrepreneur; and much of the research conducted has been based on perceptual responses rather than objective measurements. Hornaday and Aboud made attempts to develop and identify objective tests which were valid and which would not require administration by a psychologist. They found that the achievement scale of the Edwards Personal Preference Schedule and the Support, Independence, and Leadership scales of the Gordon Survey of Interpersonal Values held promise for distinguishing between entrepreneurs.[8]

Decarlo and Lyons conducted research using Hornaday and Aboud's findings as a guide. They compared selected personal characteristics of minority and non-minority female entrepreneurs. The characteristics on which noticeable differences occurred were:[9]

- Age of entrepreneur--The minority females were somewhat older than their non-minority counterparts.

- Age at the time of starting a business--The minority females reported they started their businesses at a later age than non-minority females.

- Previous entrepreneurial effort--Almost twice as many minority females as non-minority females reported that their current businesses were not their first entrepreneurial effort.

- Marriage rate--A greater proportion of the non-minority females reported never having been married. This is contrary to the 1975 Census data that reported half again as many black women as white women had never been married.

- Educational experience--A greater proportion of non-minority females reported having graduated from both high school and college. Both groups reported a higher education level than the Census had reported for all females in 1975. According to the Census, only 64 percent of all females over age 25 had completed four years of high school or more. The minority females, however,

57

reported being more active than non-minority females in extracurricular activities and were responsible for personally financing their college educations.

- Acceptance regimentation--A much greater percentage of minority females reported a willingness to accept regimentation than did the non-minority females. This may reflect the fact that female entrepreneurs represent a distinct minority in the business world.

- Means of starting a business--The minority women were much more likely than the non-minority women to have started their businesses alone than with a partner.

When non-minority female entrepreneurs were compared to minority female entrepreneurs on the nine scales of achievement, autonomy, aggression, support, conformity, recognition, independence, benevolence, and leadership, it was found that significant differences existed on six of the nine scales. The non-minority females placed a higher value on the scales of achievement, support, recognition, and independence; whereas, the minority females placed a higher value on the conformity and benevolence scales.[10]

John Mancuso has studied a group of 300 entrepreneurs for several years. He has concluded that the typical successful entrepreneur can be described as follows:[11]

- The entrepreneur is the first-born child in his or her family.

- The entrepreneur is married, with a supportive spouse.

- The entrepreneur began his or her first company at the age of 30 or so.

- Entrepreneurial tendencies manifested themselves during the teenage years.

- The level of education varies among entrepreneurs. The technical entrepreneur often has a master's degree. The typical entrepreneur probably has at least a high school and probably a college degree.

- The entrepreneur's primary motivation for going into business for herself or himself is a psychological inability to work for anyone else.

- The entrepreneur's personality developed mainly in interaction with his or her father's personality.

- The successful entrepreneur is often lucky.

- The entrepreneur seeks advice, if it is needed, from other entrepreneurs, consultants, and/or college professors.

- Entrepreneurs and money providers are often in conflict.

- The entrepreneur is essentially a doer, not a planner.

- The entrepreneur assumes moderate risks, not large or small ones.

Until recently, the world of the entrepreneur was almost entirely male. This remains true; but women are entering this world more frequently than in the past, now that the opportunities are more readily available and societal values have shifted so that it is acceptable for women to want to run their own businesses. James Schreier recently studied Milwaukee female entrepreneurs who created enterprises in "non-female" businesses (that is, he ignored Mary's Beauty Shop). He judged them by the characteristics just cited (Mancuso's study) and found the following differences.[12]

1. A stronger tendency toward self-employment in the family: 70 percent of male entrepreneurs came from a family headed by an entrepreneur; 93 percent of Schreier's female entrepreneurs did.

2. Seventy-two percent of the female entrepreneurs liked school; whereas, the male entrepreneurs (non-technical) did not like it.

3. Male entrepreneurs become entrepreneurs because they cannot work for others, as evidenced by prior job history; 50 percent of the female entrepreneurs liked working for others in previous jobs.

4. More female entrepreneurs than male ones are divorced or single.

5. Entrepreneurial behavior manifested itself later in women but mainly because of lack of opportunity. For example, some city newspapers would not hire female paper carriers.

Entrepreneurs are, of course, leaders in their own businesses, so that it is significant to examine theories pertaining to successful leadership. The following section explores two leadership trait surveys. The original survey conducted in 1948 by Stogdill, a well-known authority on leadership, reviews 24 trait studies of leadership characteristics.[13]

Successful Leadership Traits

Identified traits for successful leadership include the following:

Personality, Intelligence and Ability

In reviewing the 1948 and 1970 lists of personality characteristics, it is noted that characteristics with uniformly positive findings, which appear only in the 1948 list, are **adaptability** and **strength of conviction**. Those that appear only in the 1970 list are **adjustment, aggressiveness, independence, objectivity, resourcefulness**, and **tolerance of**

stress. Characteristics that appear with positive findings in both 1948 and 1970 lists are **alertness, originality, personal integrity,** and **self-confidence.** The research consistently reports that leaders are characterized by **superior judgement, decisiveness, knowledge**, and **fluency of speech**.

Task-Oriented Characteristics

Both surveys indicate that leaders are characterized by a high need for achievement and responsibility. They tend to be very task-oriented, dependable, persistent, have initiative, and drive, and are very enterprising.

Physical Characteristics

Results of recent research suggest that leaders tend to be endowed with an abundant reserve of energy, stamina, and the ability to maintain a high rate of physical activity.

Social Characteristics

Leaders tend to be quite active in various social activities and get along well with others. Personality traits have been found to differentiate leaders from followers, successful from unsuccessful leaders, and high-level from lower-level leaders. When considered singly, the characteristics hold very little predictive or diagnostic possibilities. In combination, however, they can generate personality dynamics advantageous to the person seeking responsibilities of leadership. Examining personality, as this author has, does not imply advocating a return to the trait approach to leadership in which personality variables were treated in somewhat an isolated fashion, suggesting that each trait acted independently to determine leadership effects. The author has modified the situation approach, with traits considered in conjunction with the situation.

When Stogdill analyzed 124 studies on leadership, he found that patterns of leadership traits differ, depending on the situation. According to Stogdill, "If there are general traits which characterize leaders, the patterns of such traits are likely to vary with the leadership requirements of different situations."[14]

The various research results previously cited can generally be summarized into two categories: **characteristics** and **personal requirements** for success in small business management.

Characteristics of Successful Small Business Managers

The following list succinctly delineates characteristics that typify successful small business managers.

1. A great sense of independence and a desire to be independent of outside control,

2. A strong sense of enterprise which lends itself to a desire to use their ideas, abilities, ambitions, aspirations, and initiatives to the greatest degree;

3. Taking their families into consideration;

4. Entrance into small business by chance rather than design;

5. Guarding their time;

6. A limited formal education; and

7. An expectation for quick results.

Professional Requirements for Success in Small Business

Contained in the list which follows are professional requirements for successful small business managers.

1. Sensitivity to internal and external changes,

2. Ability to react quickly to those changes,

3. Ability to obtain accurate and useful operating and marketing information,

4. Effective use of human resources,

5. Obtaining sufficient investment capital,

8. Effective compliance with laws,

9. Thorough understanding of the peculiarities of size,

10. Gathering industry information and keeping informed, and

11. Handling "red tape" effectively.

Motivation of Entrepreneurs

One can also look at entrepreneurs in terms of motivation theories. According to Maslow's hierarchy of needs theory, individuals move from one level to the next only after lower needs have been satisfied or nearly satisfied. Accordingly, after considerable satisfaction of basic physiological needs (hunger, thirst, etc.), the typical person would next pursue safety, social, self-esteem, and finally, self-actualization needs. Research conducted by Swayne and Tucker indicates that entrepreneurs differ from the normal population. According to them, entrepreneurs seem to be strongly motivated by self-esteem and have a fairly low requirement for love, social, physiological, and safety needs.[15] Going hand in

hand with Maslow's theory and their findings regarding entrepreneurs, the true entrepreneur

will continue to start up new ventures, and new businesses and accept new challenges even

though he [or she] is financially well-off. He [or she] continues to strive for self-

actualization through new and exciting ventures; and even though the finer things in life are

enjoyed, the thrust is toward continuing entrepreneurial endeavors.[16]

David McClelland has devoted great efforts to examine a person's need for achievement.

He [or she] has developed a need for achievement (nAch) index which can be an excellent

indicator of entrepreneurial potential. Also related to nAch and entrepreneurship is the need

for power (nPow) and the need for affiliation (nAff).[17]

Successful entrepreneurs also have a strong belief in their abilities to control their own

lives. They do not feel that other people or conditions in the external environment can keep

them from doing what they want to accomplish. Julian Rotter has pioneered the development

of measures for an internal-external (I-E) scale. His method involved forced choices between

pairs of statements presented to a subject for evaluation. Possible scores range from 0

(extremely internal) to 23 (extremely external). Studies indicate that entrepreneurs score

lower than 7 while the general population scores higher on the I-E rating. The conclusion

appears to be that believing in one's ability to be successful is very important in determining

entrepreneurial potential.[18]

More women than ever before are considering entrepreneurship as a career option;

however, the majority of the women in the work force still think in terms of being the employee rather than the employer. Realizing that all women will not make good entrepreneurs, if you think you have the ability, a good business idea, or just the desire and determination to utilize your abilities to the fullest extent, you may want to consider entrepreneurship as a career option. Entrepreneurship is indeed risky and complicated and requires much dedication. It would be remiss not to say that women also face many obstacles that can make the entrepreneurial road even more difficult than working a 9-5 job or staying home. Women frequently encounter credit procurement obstacles, financial barricades, and negative attitudes from male counterparts; often lack business experience; and suffer from a lack of role models and a peer-support base, just to mention a few.

Even if you know you have a great business idea but realize that you may not have the personal qualities to make the idea become a reality by way of a business venture, do not abandon the thought of ownership yet. There are many entrepreneurial success qualities that can be learned and developed. To achieve business success, other qualities can be obtained by joining with other individuals who have the skills, abilities, expertise, or characteristics that you may be lacking. Remember, a business idea can only become a successful business with careful planning and the implementation of appropriate business knowledge, coupled with the personal characteristics necessary for small business success.

Let's now assess your skills, abilities, talents, and strengths. We all have many attributes which could be very beneficial in the world of entrepreneurship, but many of these positive traits often go overlooked and unidentified. Take time to identify all of your strengths. Your strong points could include special talents, knowledge, past experience, tenacity, determination, levelheadedness, logical thinking, standing up well under stress, good communication skills, creativity, artistry, etc.

LIST YOUR STRENGTHS
(Don't be modest)

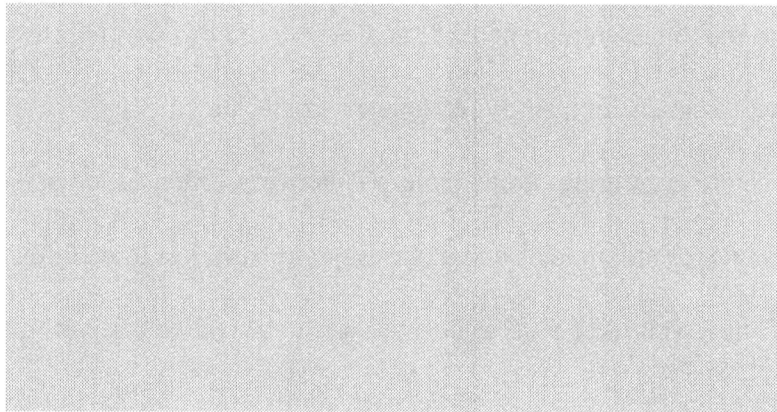

Just as you may have many personality characteristics that could help you succeed as a business owner, you may also have weaknesses which could eventually lead to entrepreneurial demise. Some of these weaknesses might include a tendency not to complete tasks you start, being more comfortable as a follower and disliking leadership responsibilities, being gullible or too kindhearted, hating to hurt someone else's feelings even though you suffer the negative consequences, being unorganized, hating details, etc. Remember, some tendencies or traits may not have been considered weaknesses before, but need to be examined now in light of the immense personal requirements necessary for success as a business owner and leader.

66

LIST YOUR WEAKNESSES
(Own up to all of them.)

Now, go back and review your strengths and weaknesses. Compare your strengths and your alterable weaknesses with the characteristics common among successful entrepreneurs. Do you have significant weaknesses? If so, can most of them be positively changed? Do you think you have what it takes for entrepreneurial success?

Before embarking on any new enterprise, potential entrepreneurs need to be in touch with themselves, their desires and their personal objectives, as well as their strengths and weaknesses. The following format should help you become more aware of your individual goals and assist you in further assessing your personal qualities relative to the characteristics common among successful female entrepreneurs.

67

LIFE PLANNING

PURPOSE: *TO SET AT LEAST TWO CLEAR GOALS FOR YOUR LIFE, TO SPECIFY PLANS OF ACTION TO REACH THOSE GOALS, AND TO HELP YOU DETERMINE IF YOU HAVE A GENUINE INTEREST IN ENTREPRENEURSHIP.*

Life Line

Use the following line to represent your life from beginning to end. Put a check mark on the line to indicate where you are now.

BIRTH_____**DEATH**

Address such questions as:

- What was the happiest year or period in your life?
- What was the turning point in your life?
- What was the lowest point in your life?
- Was there an event in your life when you demonstrated great courage?
- Was there a time of great grief?
- What peak experiences have you had? What things do you want to start doing at this point in your life?
- Was there a time when you were very enterprising?

Reflect on your feelings represented by the line before and after the check mark. What does this tell you about who you are and what you want out of life?

Typical Day

A circle will be used to depict how you spend a typical day. Divide the circle into four quarters using dotted lines. Each slice represents six hours. Now, estimate how many hours or parts of an hour you spend on each of the following areas on a typical day: SLEEP, SCHOOL, WORK, WITH FRIENDS--socializing, playing sports, etc., WITH FAMILY, ALONE--thinking, playing, reading, watching television, CHORES, MISCELLANEOUS PASTIMES, ETC.

MY TYPICAL DAY

Are you satisfied with the relative sizes of your slices?

How Would You Like Your Ideal Day To Look?

Ideally, how big would you want each slice to be? Draw your ideal pie.

MY IDEAL DAY

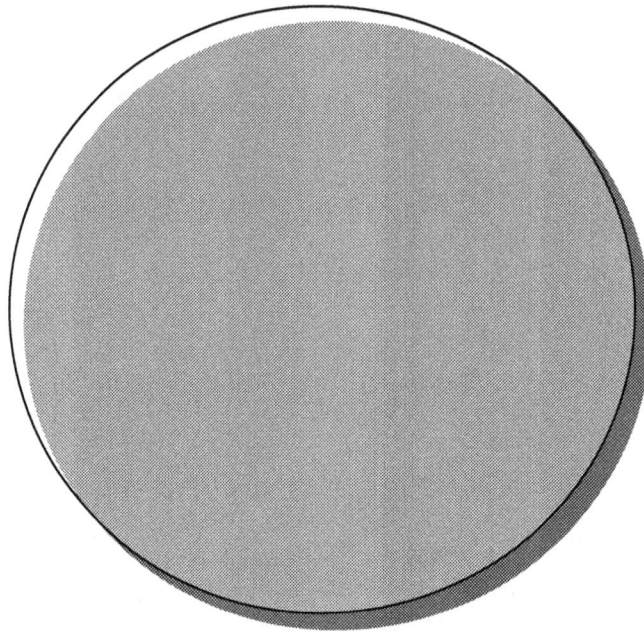

Realistically, is there anything you can do to begin to change the size of some of your slices to the desired sizes?

SHORT-TERM AND LONG-TERM GOALS

Capture a vision of you operating a successful business in the thriving crafts industry or art arena. What products are you selling? What is the name of your successful business? How many employees do you have? How many customers or clients do you have on a daily and monthly basis? How much money are you making monthly? What type of revenue and profit do you expect to realize in the future? Is the phone ringing off the hook with new orders? Are you bombarded by e-mail for orders and even public speaking engagements? Do you have so many orders that you have to hire employees? Are orders flowing in on your Web site? Are you overwhelmed by on-line orders from an auction or direct buy service? Are you operating from a new facility, a new studio, or from the comfort of your home or even a new home? The possibilities go on and on. What type of lifestyle do you want to create? Capture your vision and write it down.

<u>MY VISION</u>

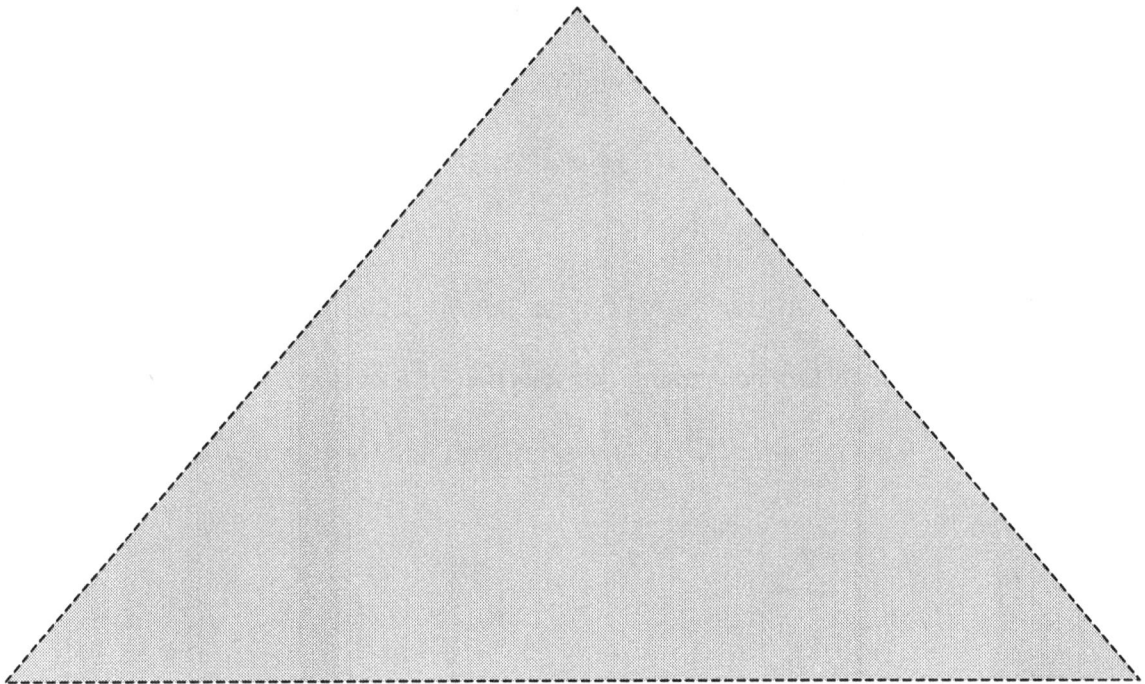

Now, let's translate your vision into short-term and long-term goals. At the same time, consider how much time will be required to achieve your goals? How much work will be required? Will your family be supportive or will conflicts arise? Sometimes you even need to consider subconscious jealousy and/or competition from your spouse or significant other and the negative repercussions. You may also run into the double bind of taking so much of your time to make your business a success and achieving the income that comes along with success that when you realize the fruits of your labor and have extra money to enjoy life through vacations and family fun, you don't have time to really enjoy yourself because you have to constantly devote more time to keeping the business successful, and/or you find that your mind is constantly on the business. This is one of the drawbacks of success. In essence, when you consider your goals, you may want to consciously limit your growth, based on your values, priorities, and personal situation. This is a major consideration that should be addressed at the initiation of a business.

Make sure that you set realistic goals and expectations of yourself and your business. If your goals are too high, you will quickly find yourself discouraged and frustrated. Conservative business goals will allow you to be exuberant and more motivated when you do better than you anticipated. Make sure you have prioritized your goals, assessed all drawbacks, and know what really makes you happy. Consider all of these factors as we proceed to the next section concerning the selection of a business that's right for you. But first take some time and write down your short-term and long-term goals. Make sure you attach a specific time frame to each goal.

SHORT-TERM GOALS

LONG-TERM GOALS

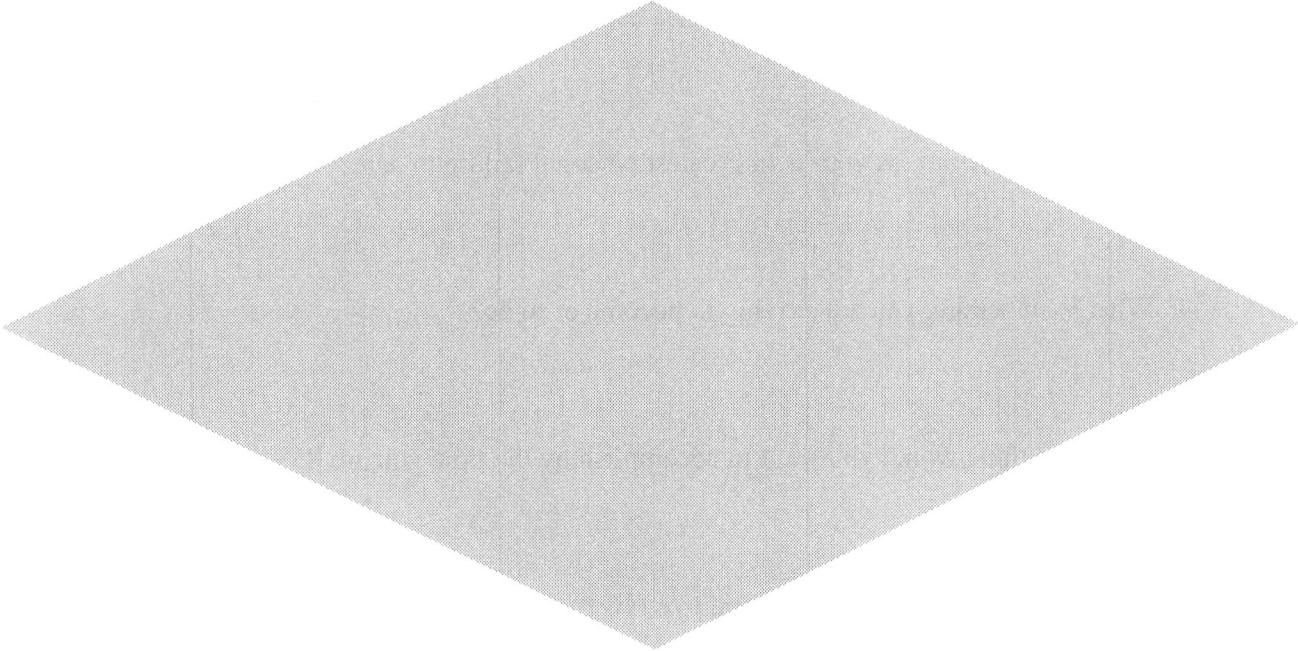

73

SELF-AWARENESS

This section involves looking at yourself by way of developing a coat of arms as seen on the following page. This should help you address the following considerations: WHAT AM I DOING WITH MY LIFE? AM I JUST REACTING TO OTHERS, OR AM I IN CONTROL OF THE DIRECTION OF MY LIFE? IS MY LIFE MAKING A DIFFERENCE? AM I JUST SETTLING FOR WHATEVER COMES MY WAY?

Answer each of the questions below by drawing in the appropriate area on the coat of arms on the following page. Use pictures, designs, or symbols. Do not use words except in area six.

1. What do you regard as your greatest personal achievement to date?

2. What do you regard as your family's greatest achievement?

3. What do you regard as your own greatest personal failure to date?

4. What is something you are striving to become or to be?

5. What one thing would you want to accomplish by the time you are 85?

6. What is the personal motto by which you live?

COAT OF ARMS

What would you most like to accomplish in your lifetime?

Write for two minutes, without stopping, in the space provided below. (Make sure to reflect on all aspects of your life, including family, finances, and the physical, social, spiritual, love, and intellectual components of your life.)

76

You will need to thoroughly assess your likes and dislikes about work. The total responsibility of the business rests on the shoulders of the business owner. The business owner will need to be prepared to do all of the tasks required to keep the business going. Even though you may hire people to do the tasks you might dislike, such as bookkeeping, there will come a time when you will have to pitch in and help or do it all, either because of employee absence from work or because of cost-cutting considerations. In the beginning, you may be working with limited capital and may have to do everything yourself. Make sure that you are mentally prepared to cope with having to perform "hated" tasks.

LIKES AND DISLIKES ABOUT JOBS/WORK

LIKES   DISLIKES

1.   1.

2.   2.

3.   3.

4.   4.

5.   5.

6.   6.

7.   7.

REVIEW

Look back over your responses and address the following:

1. What do you want in your future?

2. You may find that priorities for your desires and goals have emerged. Set dates for accomplishments. You may have discovered hidden interests. Include the type of business you may want to start if business ownership is part of your desires.

3. How do your personal characteristics rate compared to those of successful entrepreneurs?

HOW DO YOU PLAN TO GET THERE?

What resources do you have to help you achieve these goals?

What training or experience is needed to achieve these goals?

What things do you want or need to start doing less? More?

Are your life goals oriented toward owning and operating your own business? What type? What leads you to your conclusions?

SELECTING THE TYPE OF BUSINESS TO ENTER

Even though the number of female-owned businesses is increasing, the success of these ventures is not guaranteed. Successful ventures can only occur with careful planning and the execution of good business and management principles and practices, coupled with the existence of necessary personal factors on the part of the business owner.

Approximately 55 percent of all small business failures are due partially, if not entirely, to the lack of managerial ability and experience.[17] Certainly, therefore, managerial knowledge and ability are necessary for success in small business. This publication will provide the basic knowledge necessary for starting and operating a small business. It should be noted that management ability includes the personal requirements necessary for success which can often be overlooked when evaluating the reason a certain business is successful or unsuccessful. Entrepreneurial success depends significantly on the existence of strong personal entrepreneurial requirements and not business knowledge alone. This publication, therefore, also presents significant information concerning entrepreneurial characteristics as well as managerial knowledge. The information presented allows the reader to conduct an analysis to determine whether the possible business is, in fact, a feasible venture and whether it has a chance for success. At the same time, the information also allows the reader to develop a business plan for the venture.

BACKGROUND

There is not any consistent definition for a small business. Some of the small business literature uses a definition such as a firm having a name, an owner, and one or more workers other than the owner. Using such a broad definition, approximately 95 percent of all businesses can be considered small. The Small Business Administration (SBA), the governmental agency directing efforts toward small business, defines a small business as a business independently owned and operated, and not dominant in its field. The SBA goes further to categorize firms as being small by way of certain criteria such as number of employees and dollar volume of business. One really has to develop a feel for what a small business is. Generally, if one is starting a new business, it can be assumed that it will be considered small initially. Small business offers many benefits. Small firms tend:

1. To be more in touch with employees, thereby encouraging better employee relations;

2. To be more in touch with customers and are able to provide more personal service;

3. To provide almost half of all jobs;

4. To help insure competition;

5. To provide jobs for the disadvantaged and ethnic groups;

6. To help expand the economy;

7. To provide workers and owners with wider learning experiences;

8. To provide personal rewards (i.e., financial security or wealth, personal satisfaction, and, what is considered a major advantage by many, independence).

The problems encountered by small businesses are many. The disadvantages and pitfalls of small business include the following:

- Fewer opportunities to make costly mistakes (One major mistake, such as purchasing the wrong inventory, can cause failure.);

- Inadequate funds to employ managerial assistance or consulting help;

- Shortage of working capital;

- Poor record-keeping systems;

- Lack of effective selling techniques;

- No marketing research;

- Inability to cope with growth problems;

- Lack of experience of many entrepreneurs;

- Poor location selection;

- Too much inventory, particularly the wrong kind;

- Excessive purchase of fixed assets, such as elaborate buildings when first starting;

- Poor credit-granting policies;

- Unwarranted personal expenditures;

- Unplanned expansions.

Given the many pitfalls of small business, the failure rate of small businesses is extraordinarily high. Half of the businesses started each year fail. Half of the businesses that fail do so during the first five years of operation. Nine out of ten failures are traceable to managerial inexperience and incompetence. Other reasons for business failures include too little capital, poor organization, obsolescence of service or product, obsolescence of equipment, poor personnel practices, and inappropriate personal characteristics.

At this point, you should have determined that you have or can develop the personal characteristics required for success as an entrepreneur and that you truly want to take the entrepreneurial challenge. We now need to put those success traits into action and start developing your business.

Types of Businesses

By virtue of the fact that you are reading this book, you have probably already decided that you want to start a craft shop. However, the type of business you enter will be influenced by your personal value system, education, training, financial ability, and family situation, as well as by your particular interests and desires.

Small businesses can be categorized into six types:

1. retailing,   4. research and development,

2. service,   5. consulting, and

3. wholesaling,   6. manufacturing.

You must start with a business idea and develop your business or venture from there. Before making a preliminary analysis of the market, production, or financial aspects of your venture, you must be able to describe and define your business concept. An idea for a business must address a need of an identified market which is presently not satisfied and, at the same time, be innovative enough to attract people to your product or service as opposed to the competition. It is important to be innovative enough to attract customers; but if your service or product is too unusual, it may take too long for people to accept it. Consequently, your business will fail while you attempt to make people aware of the need for your product or service. Remember that the type of business you enter will be influenced by your personal value system, education, training, financial ability, and your family situation, as well as by your particular interests and desires.

In selecting a business, you should address the following major questions:

1. What type of business do you think you might want to enter? Why?

2. Exactly what products and/or services should be sold?

3. Who will be the primary customer groups for your product or service?

4. What are the eventual uses for your product or service by the customer?

5. Why will customers want to buy your product or service? (Ask yourself questions which identify the key benefits or advantages of your product or service to the customer, such as lower price, better quality, etc.)

6. What in fact is your total product? (List everything you will be offering to your customers, not only the physical.)

ASSESSING YOUR MONETARY REQUIREMENTS

The question that is probably running through your mind is how much money is needed to get the business started and keep it operating? This question cannot be addressed without first taking an in-depth look at the total venture you're considering. All of the information obtained can then be compiled in a business plan format. Below you will find factors that will need to be addressed in determining start-up and operating costs. This information is presented in brief in this section. It is presented at this time so that you will be conscious of significant cost centers as we begin working on preparing a business plan for your venture. Capital requirements will be addressed in a more detailed worksheet format as a part of the business plan preparation process in Chapter III.

The amount of money you will need to start your business depends on many factors. The following are major factors you need to take into consideration in determining your monetary requirements:

- The type of business being established,

- The location of the business,

- The sales volume anticipated,

- How quickly the sales volume desired can be obtained,

- Whether you buy or lease the facilities in which the business will be operating,

- How extensive the product line is,

- Whether the business will operate on a cash basis or extend credit,

- How much money the entrepreneur has to invest in the business,

- How much legal assistance is needed,

- The cost of preparing the business facility for use,

- The cost of store fixtures and equipment,

- The amount and cost of the beginning inventory,

- The cost of establishing an accounting system and the forms required,

- The cost of personnel,

- The cost of delivering merchandise to customers and inventory to the business,

- The cost of licenses and permits,

- The cost of utilities,

- The cost of insurance,

- Advertising expenses, and

- The amount of money deposited in a reserve fund to take care of business and personal expenses until your business turns a profit.

All of these factors have been taken into consideration in the preparation of the cost worksheets that follow. As we work on the preparation of your business plan, you will be able to insert certain costs when they are considered.

START-UP COSTS

Start-up costs include all of the expenses your business will incur in preparation for opening. Major cost areas are presented below; however, you will need to alter the sample form, based on the specifics of your business. Some of the expenses listed will be one-time-only costs or expenses you incur once a year. Other expenses will occur monthly.

BUSINESS ORGANIZATIONAL EXPENSES	MONTHLY	YEARLY
Start-up inventory		
Facility costs		
Decorating and remodeling		
Furniture		
Professional and legal fees		
Franchise fee, if applicable		
Licenses and permits		
Telephone installation		
Telephone services		
Telephone answering service		
Insurance		
Personnel		
Deposits for utilities		
Installation of fixtures		
TOTAL		
ADVERTISING AND PROMOTIONAL EXPENSES		
Business cards		
Mailers, posters, ads		
Business logo design		
Signs (outdoor)		
Bags		
Other		
TOTAL		
OFFICE OPERATING EXPENSES		
Stationery		
Invoice forms		
Purchase order forms		
Computer service costs		
Pens, pencils, misc.		
Tables & Equipment		
Other		
TOTAL		

FURNITURE AND FIXTURES		
Desks and chairs		
Filing cabinets		
Wastebaskets		
Safe		
Copying machine		
Adding machine		
Storage shelves		
Cabinets		
Computers & Technology		
Office furniture		
Lighting		
Display cases		
TOTAL		
BUSINESS VEHICLE		
REAL ESTATE		
EQUIPMENT		
OWNER'S LIVING EXPENSES		
Home mortgage payments or rent		
Food		
Home repair and maintenance		
Outstanding debts (Credit cards, etc,)		
Loans		
Entertainment		
Education		
Auto and repair		
Furniture		
Clothing		
Travel		
Taxes		
Utilities		
Medical expenses		
Insurance costs		
Other		
TOTAL		
TOTAL PERSONAL EXPENSES		
Subtract outside income yet to be obtained while running the business.		
TOTAL PERSONAL EXPENSES TO BE COVERED BY THE BUSINESS		

EVALUATING YOUR MONETARY REQUIREMENTS

Prior to approaching a lending institution or investors for assistance in funding your business, you will need to make sure you have the answers to the following questions:

1. How much money do you need?

2. What exactly do you need the money for? Some specific reasons for needing money include buying equipment, supplies, renting space, salaries, money to meet financial obligations to suppliers, etc.

3. What collateral do you have? What do you or your business own which can be offered as security for money received?

4. When do you need the money?

5. How long do you need the money?

6. Can you afford the cost of the money?

7. Where can you find the money? (Make sure you have backups in place.)

REMEMBER, IT IS BETTER TO OVERESTIMATE THAN UNDERESTIMATE YOUR FINANCIAL REQUIREMENTS!!

The answers to all of these questions and other major business considerations should be summarized in a coherent, precise written format. This information constitutes a business plan and is discussed in the following chapter.

"Three Critical Keys to Entrepreneurial Success:

PASSION, PLANNING, AND PERSEVERANCE."

M.G.L.J.

CHAPTER III

THE BUSINESS PLAN

"The successful entrepreneur starts with a vision and passionately details a plan to bring the vision to fruition."

M.G.L.J.

THE BUSINESS PLAN

A business plan is a report written by the initiator of a business which describes the venture in detail--**WHAT** business you are in, **WHO** will be active in it, **WHY** you believe it will be successful, and **HOW** you intend to implement your plans. The business plan should be prepared with great care and thought and should be concise, readable, well written, and substantive.

From an internal perspective, the business plan forces the business owner to write down all of his or her thoughts and researched data pertaining to the business. Many considerations would go unaddressed, and many thoughts and ideas would never be captured again if it were not for the business plan. The business plan is also crucial because it serves as a checklist and timetable for accomplishing stated objectives.

Externally, the business plan is used to attract financial as well as human resources. Lending institutions and investors want to be able to examine your organized plans to determine if your venture has merit and whether it warrants their investment. The business plan can also be used to attract key personnel and business partners, as well as serve as a means to communicate to others what your business is about. Even many small business consulting firms and assistance offices will ask you for a business plan prior to rendering any type of service. A GOOD BUSINESS PLAN IS CRUCIAL!

A good business plan will consist of, but is not limited to, the following major informational areas.

The Business

- Detailed description of the business including name, location, business goals and objectives, industry information and assessment, economic trends, etc.;

- Description of the product (services and/or goods), potential of product line, technology, and possible advances;

- Description of the marketing plan, including target market, marketing strategies, channels of distribution, market size and share, market potential, pricing strategy, and promotion;

- Assessment of competition;

- Management, covering such areas as key personnel, names of accountants, lawyers, consultants, organizational structure, experience of key personnel, educational background and experience;

- Legal structure, describing the proprietorship, partnership, or corporation;

- Personnel, listing personnel requirements, position descriptions, labor trends, and compensation;

- Facilities and equipment;

- Sources of supply;

- Critical risks and problems;

- Economic trends; and

- Strategies for the future.

Financial Data

- Capital equipment,

- Sources of funds,

- Balance sheet,

- Break-even analysis,

- Income projections or profit-loss statement,

- Pro forma cash flow,

- Uses of funds, and

- Desired funding.

Supporting Documents

- Resumes of key personnel,

- Personal financial statements,

- Credit reports,

- Letters of reference,

- Copies of leases,

- Contracts,

- Legal documents,

- Drawings,

- Photographs,

- Articles, and

- Any additional pertinent information.

The following worksheets are provided to help you organize your thoughts regarding your business. The remaining format of this publication will present crucial information necessary for starting a craft or art business followed by questions for you to address. The summarization of the answers to these questions will be important components of your business plan. Upon completion of this publication, you should have your business plan in good order.

Now that you have a feel for what is included in a completed business plan, continue reading the next chapter on start-up costs. It will become obvious that in order to fill in most of these blanks, substantial investigatory work will have to be done on your part. In fact, these blanks will need to be filled in, as well as the questions answered from the previous section on your financial needs, before you near the completion of your plan. All of these questions need to be kept in mind throughout the business plan preparation process.

BUSINESS PLAN WORKSHEETS

The importance of a well-conceived business plan cannot be stressed enough. The business plan outline covers the major topics to be considered in the planning process. Experience has revealed that most mistakes or failures of businesses occur not from bad information, but from a lack of information. The business plan, among other things, helps you to determine if you have sufficient information, capital, and customers to initiate your venture. As stated earlier, the business plan is immensely important in requesting a bank loan or any form of financing or assistance. Even an advertising consultant will ask to see your business plan before attempting to map out an advertising program for your firm. These worksheets are designed in such a way that you can simply fill in the blanks and have a basic narrative for all business plan components. As you proceed with this publication, insert the appropriate information in the spaces provided. Also, make sure you insert appropriate amounts on your cost sheets. Upon completion of the publication, you should have completed your business plan and have it ready to be typed.

BUSINESS PLAN

NAME OF THE BUSINESS _____

Be sure the name is distinctive, will stick in the minds of your customers or clients, and accurately describes the nature of your business. Also check to make sure that no one else is using the name or a very similar name, particularly in the same industry.

Check with your state trademark office and register your business name. This is usually not very expensive, but be sure to include the amount on your cost sheet. You may also want to register your business name and logo, that is, the symbol that you use to identify your business, with the Federal Trademark Office. If you are having trouble coming up with a name, don't belabor the point. A good name will probably come to you as you continue your investigatory work into the industry.

LOCATION In light of the selected target market and after reflecting on many major

location considerations,_____ will be strategically
(name of business)

located at:_____.

This location was selected because. . . . .

Take time to thoroughly assess your location options and reflect on the information presented in this section of the manual. Make sure you have considered such factors as the pros and cons of a post office box, your business image, operating out of a home office, and accessibility to your target market, as well as cost factors. (See Chapter VII.)

TELEPHONE

Make sure you have a business listing in the phone book even if you are operating out of the home. Your accessibility by phone is very important. If you cannot afford a secretary, use an answering service. Avoid answering machines if at all possible. They are a turn-off to most people. Don't forget to include your business telephone and answering service costs on your cost sheets.

STATEMENT OF PURPOSE AND NATURE OF BUSINESS:

_____

_____

_____

_____

WHAT IS THE PURPOSE OF YOUR BUSINESS? WHAT MARKET ARE YOU AIMING FOR? WHY ARE YOU IN BUSINESS? THIS SHOULD BE A SUCCINCT STATEMENT PERTAINING TO WHAT YOUR BUSINESS IS ALL ABOUT.

EXAMPLE: "A BUSINESS OF YOUR OWN" is a multi-faceted service firm established to assist women in starting and managing small businesses. "A BUSINESS OF YOUR OWN" specializes in business start-up publications and auxiliary services to assist the female small business owner and aspiring owner. "A BUSINESS OF YOUR OWN" publications range from general start-up manuals to more specific manuals with information about starting particular businesses. "A BUSINESS OF YOUR OWN'S" goal is to assist women in pulling together the intricate components necessary to make their small businesses successful.

Industry Overview Examine the industry your business is in, including national, regional, and local standpoints. Create a narrative which will address historical and concrete growth projections along with the number of local and national firms. Discuss how your venture fits into the industry context and indicate factors that will give your business the competitive edge in the marketplace, based on industry information. Much industry information can be obtained from the local library, trade associations and trade publications, and from Web sites. Be sure to check the appendix of this manual for useful informational sources.

Form of Ownership _____ is a _____.
                              name of business   form of ownership

99

Discuss the form of legal ownership (proprietorship, partnership, or corporation) your business will use and why. (See Chapter V.)

Marketing   Discuss your **target market**. Use results from your research to justify the appropriateness of your market.   Cite published information which supports your target market selection.   Discuss in detail your "total product," including auxiliary services, packaging, warranties, delivery service, repairs, installation, guarantees, etc.   Detail your promotion plans for attracting customers or clients, penetrating your target market, and getting repeat customers.   Again, do not forget to insert all of your marketing expenses on the cost sheets. Discuss how your product will be **distributed** and/or how services will be performed.   What type of market penetration do you hope to obtain and when?   What is the **pricing** structure for your products and services?   Make sure you can show legitimate justification for all of your business decisions, and make sure you are being consistent with your image and product positioning.   (See Chapter IV.)

The selected target market for _____ is
                                            (name of business)

_____. This market was determined to be appropriate after
(target market)

conducting marketing research.   _____ individuals were surveyed for the purpose
                                        (# people)

of_____and to determine if the originally identified

target market would be receptive to the business idea. The survey findings are presented in

the appendix.

The product of _____ is presently in the
(name of business)

_____ stage of development. The product has
(introduction, growth, maturity)

many strengths including _____. In spite of the

many strengths of the business's products/services, certain weaknesses have been

identified. These weaknesses are as follows: _____. The

identified weaknesses will be overcome by _____.
(action to be taken)

To inform and persuade customers/clients to patronize _____,
(name of business)

a varied promotional strategy will be employed. This strategy will include

_____
(types of promotion)

Distribution of the product or service will be achieved by _____.

A _____ pricing strategy will be used. This was decided
(penetration/skimming)   (Note: See page 117)

because_____

_____.

Competition The strengths of the competition will be overcome by...........

WHO ARE YOUR MAJOR COMPETITORS? WHAT SHARE OF THE MARKET DO

THEY PRESENTLY HAVE? WHAT ARE THEIR STRENGTHS AND WEAKNESSES?

HOW WILL YOU OVERCOME THEIR STRENGTHS AND OBTAIN A VIABLE SHARE

OF THE MARKET? WHAT SHARE OF THE MARKET DO YOU HOPE TO OBTAIN

AND WHEN?

Research indicated that there are _____ major immediate
(# of competitors)

competitors. The major competitors are: _____,_____,

_____,_____,and _____. They have

_____, _____, _____ and _____ percent shares of the market respectively.

COMPETITOR ANALYSIS

Competitor Name	Strengths	Weaknesses

Personnel Discuss all of your personnel requirements. Discuss all of the activities that will

be necessary in order for your firm to accomplish its objectives, and then discuss the type of

people you plan to hire to complete these activities. Make sure to address qualifications,

compensation plans, and any other major personnel considerations. Discuss the key

management personnel, with particular attention being paid to their experience in the

102

industry and their qualifications. Attach resumes for all key personnel. Devote a separate section to addressing the qualifications of the business owner. Don't fail to include a narrative about your success qualities which were discussed and assessed earlier in this manual.

Initially, _____ will have _____.
                     (name of business)   (# employees)

They will hold the following positions and have the following responsibilities:

Position	Responsibilities

Personnel will be compensated based on _____.
                                               (salary, hourly wage)

Key Personnel The key personnel are (include yourself):

Their qualifications and functions are as follows:

Position	Qualifications	Functions

Organizational Structure After you have determined the types of activities necessary to fulfill your organization's objectives, you can determine the most logical way for these

103

activities to interact within the confines of the organization. Who does what? Who is accountable to whom? Diagram your organizational structure. Initially, the organizational structure may only consist of you, but think about growth planning.

Production   Describe the facilities necessary to house the operations of your business. Discuss any lease or purchase arrangements and all facility improvement plans along with costs for these arrangements and plans. Re-examine the rationale for your selection of the facility and the lease or purchase decision.

If you are producing a product or service, discuss production in detail. Address inventory and quality control considerations as well as costs.

Facilities

Initially,_____ will be housed in _____.
                        (name of business)   (describe facility)

The facility consists of. . . . .

Equipment

Explain in detail and list all required equipment, fixtures, etc. Assess the costs and discuss the purchase and lease arrangements and payment terms.

Supplies

List all of your supply requirements including the names of the suppliers and the terms of payment. Assess the reasoning behind the selection of a supplier. Include delivery time, order quantities, and backup sources for all supplies.

Insurance

List insurance coverage to be carried on your business facility, equipment, officers, and liability coverage.

Accounting Firm

Discuss your selection of an accounting firm, the services the accountants will be performing, and the costs for these services. Include the address of the accounting firm.

The business will use the accounting services of _____.
(name of accounting firm)

Their services have been obtained because _____.

They will provide the following services _____.

Banks/Financial Institutions

_____

_____

_____

Legal Counsel

Discuss services to be performed and costs.

_____

_____

_____

Critical Risks and Problems

_____

_____

_____

Growth Plans

_____

_____

_____

Financial Information

The next step is to translate your business plan into dollars. Make sure to include profit/loss forecasts, pro forma balance sheets, cash flow projections, and break-even analysis. (See Chapter XI and Glosssary)

Make sure that you have inserted all of the pertinent cost information on your cost sheets and that you have transferred these items to the appropriate financial statements.

Thoroughly assess your capital requirements necessary to get your business off the ground and running for at least one year.

Appendix

Provide Support Documentation (including, but not limited to, the following):

- Resumes of Key Personnel

- Personal Financial Statements

- Credit Reports

- Letters of Reference

- Copies of Leases (if applicable)

- Contracts (if applicable)

- Legal Documents

- Insurance Policies

- Partnership Agreements or Corporation Charter (if applicable)

- Patents

- Copyrights

- Trademarks

- Buy/Sell Contract

- Promotional Material

- Photographs (if deemed appropriate)

- Brochures (or other promotional documents)

"The best business plan ever written becomes

futile effort if there is no execution.

You must be prepared to "get off of go."

M.G.L.J.

CHAPTER IV

MARKETING

"The entrepreneur is a walking and talking billboard

for her business.

You must present a professional appearance at all times,

even in the grocery store."

M.G.L.J.

MARKETING

Regardless of the type of business one selects to start, there will be a product or service that needs to be sold or marketed to the public. Contrary to old beliefs of production orientation where firms decided what they wanted to make and then attempted to sell the product, it is advisable for firms to adhere to the marketing-orientation concept. This concept holds that firms should seek to satisfy their customers at a profit. This involves determining the needs and wants of a selected customer group first, and then attempting to satisfy their desires. Encompassed here is the selection of a **target market**, a group of individuals to whom you want to direct your efforts and attempt to satisfy, followed by the manipulation of what is called the **marketing mix** to satisfy this target market. The **marketing mix** (or the 4 P's), include the **product, price, place,** and **promotion**. In other words, you must come up with the right product, at the right price, at the right place, and use the right promotion to satisfy the chosen target market. The "four P's" are explained in the following sections.

Product

The product component of the marketing mix includes not only the specific good or service offered for sale, but also its reputation, name, packaging, image, as well as the accompanying services and any innovative services. The product of a craft business, in fact, does not have to be physical at all but could be the rendering of related services such as delivery and original design for custom orders.

The beauty of the product is also an important component of a marketing strategy. The visual appeal of your product will bring you additional customers when others marvel at your

111

creative designs and your overall presentation of the product. Therefore, the total product offered by a firm may include a large array of goods as well as related services such as parking facilities and credit. Total product planning is obviously crucial in order to provide the "right" product for the selected target market. Total product planning needs to encompass cognition of **product life cycles**. Like humans, products go through life cycles. The **life cycle** of products is generally divided into several stages: **product introduction, market growth, market maturity, sales decline, and product termination.**

The **introduction stage** involves informing the target market of the existence of the product or service as well as its advantages and uses. During the introductory stage, a great deal of money is spent on promoting the product. The business may experience losses since money invested in the business at this point is also for future benefits.

During the **growth stage**, the business owner will begin to make a profit. As other firms or individuals see the entrepreneur making money, they will try to imitate the product. Competition, therefore, becomes strong during this phase.

During the **market maturity stage**, many competitors have entered the market. Competition may be very fierce and could cause profits to decline. Advertising, thus, becomes very important. This phase, as well as the other stages, could last for any period of time.

During the **sales decline phase,** new products begin to replace the old. If a firm sees its "total" product moving into the sales decline phase, intense planning needs to be conducted to alter the product or even change products or the nature of the business before sales decline

112

significantly. However, product planning needs to be conducted continuously so as to avoid getting into the sales decline predicament. Entrepreneurs must be ever conscious of their environment to be prepared to change direction or alter strategies and/or products quickly.

The **product termination phase** involves the termination of product sales because a market no longer exists for the product, or the product is obsolete because of new technological advances or alternative choices formerly not available.

Surveying the Market for Product Marketability

You need to see if your perception of the need for your product or service is the same as your identified customer group, or target market, which you wish to serve. At this point, an interview of constituents in your target market should be conducted to determine whether your identified customer group desires your product or service, or whether your business idea is satisfying any need except your need to be in business for yourself.

A brief questionnaire should be drawn up and presented either verbally or in written form. Questions should be designed to give you specific answers, but at the same time open enough for respondents to possibly give you some ideas for product or service changes when they respond. The sample questionnaire which follows should serve as a guide in designing a survey for your business idea. Be sure to survey as many individuals as possible who are in your target market.

Sample Questionnaire

We are conducting a survey to determine the desire for a craft and art business in the Atlanta area offering various unique handcrafted items and works of art. Please be kind enough to answer the following brief questions.

1. Where do you presently purchase your handcrafted and art items?

(Mark all that apply)

- o   Don't purchase any
- o   Craft fairs
- o   Art shows
- o   Local craft store (Please indicate store and its location) _____
- o   Internet
- o   Gift shop (please indicate shop and its location)_____
- o   Art gallery
- o   Flower shop (please indicate shop you frequent and its location)_____
- o   Church bazaar or other non-profit event
- o   Other_____

2. Were you satisfied with your purchases? (Yes/No)_____. If you were not satisfied, what displeased you?_____

3. What features would make a craft and art store offering unique handcrafted items attractive to you?

(Mark all that apply)

o Selection of items	o Delivery service
o Quality of products	o Reputation of artisan
o Uniqueness of items offered	o Internet services and sales availability
o Nostalgic craft items	o Gift wrapping
o Convenience to work	o Gift reminder service (store contacts you
o Convenience to home	about an upcoming birthday, anniversary
o Shopping mall location	or special annual occasion).
o Cost of items	o Other_____
o Personal service and attention	

4. In what types of art and crafts are you generally interested?

(Mark all that apply)

o Ceramics	o Craft items for children's rooms
o Pottery	o Craft items for the bath
o Candles	o Handcrafted items for the bedroom (e.g.
o Decoupage	bedspreads, quilts, throw pillows, linens)
o Original art work	o Crafts for the kitchen
o Art prints (signed and numbered)	o Needlework
o Hand tufted rugs	o Stuffed animals
o Holiday crafts	o Gift baskets
o Primitive crafts	o Wearable art
o Folk art	o Brass gift items
o Unique throw pillows	o Oriental gift items
o Hand woven items	o Porcelain/crystal gift items

o Country crafts	o Silver gift items	
o Stained glass	o Jewelry	
o Furniture	o Other _____	
o Lamps		

5. For which occasions are you most likely to purchase art and handcrafted items?

(Mark all that apply)

o For Self	o Corporate Gifts
o Birthday Gift	o Love and Romance
o Get Well Gift	o Thank You Gift
o Mother's Day	o Thinking of You Gift
o Father's Day	o Congratulations Gift
o Sympathy Gift	o Other _____
o Wedding Gift	

6. In what price range do you expect to pay for a handcrafted item?

o Under $25	o $65 - 84 _____
o $25 - 44 _____	o $85 or above _____
o $45 - 64 _____	

7. In what price range do you expect to pay for an original work of art?

o $100 - 199 _____	o $300 - 399 _____
o $200 - 299 _____	o $400 or above _____

8. Please provide the following information about yourself.

Sex ____M ____F   Ethnic Background _____

Married ____ Single ____   Occupation _____
Household income range: Rent _____ Own Home _____
    under $40,000 _____

    $40,001-60,000 ____

    $60,001-80,000 ____   Section of city where you reside:_____

    $80,001-90,000 ____   Section of city where you do most of your
                                        art and craft shopping: _____
    above $90,000 _____

9. Would you patronize an art and craft boutique located at_____?

{Insert where you are thinking about locating.}

Thank you so very much for your time and your responses.

Evaluate your questionnaire responses. Does the result of the questionnaire information indicate that your target market desires the product you offer? Does your target market need to be changed or widened? Does your total service/product need changing?

It must now be determined whether the service offered is technically feasible, whether it could achieve a competitive advantage, and if the cost and time necessary for development are worthwhile.

A. Status

1. What is the current stage of development of the venture's service (introduction, maturity, etc.)? Is there something that gives your service a "new twist" in the minds of the public?

If the service needs licenses, indicate which ones and all the procedures necessary for obtaining them. Also indicate all permits or certificates as applicable.

2. What must be done to get the service ready for sale? Think in terms of the total product and packaging.

B. Strengths and Weaknesses

Strengths

1. Indicate any patents or trademarks on your service. Do these give you a competitive advantage?

116

2. What design features of your service give it an advantage over the competition?

3. What is your estimate of the life expectancy of your service?

<u>Weaknesses</u>

1. Are there any features of your service that may put it at a disadvantage in the marketplace?

2. Indicate any possibilities of rapid change in demand because of population trends and/or developments, such as an increased number of new competitors.

Price

Price is another one of the "four P's" which the entrepreneur can adjust to satisfy the target market. A pricing strategy must be developed. The entrepreneur must determine whether products generally will be priced higher, lower, or the same as the competition. Initially, the products could be offered at a price lower than the competition's to obtain a high sales volume, with prices raised later **(penetration pricing)**; or the products could be offered initially at a high price and lowered later **(skimming pricing)**. The entrepreneur also has the task of determining the specific price of all products and/or services. With pricing the product or service, there are many factors to consider. Included are: channel of distribution used, competition's pricing strategy, annual anticipated sales volume, product life cycle, opportunity for special promotions, the image of the product, and operation expenses.

Place

A major part of place considerations is the determination of the appropriate channel of distribution to use for the product to get to the target market. There are four basic channels of distribution that the entrepreneur may want to consider, and of course, there are many variations of the four.

BASIC CHANNELS OF DISTRIBUTION

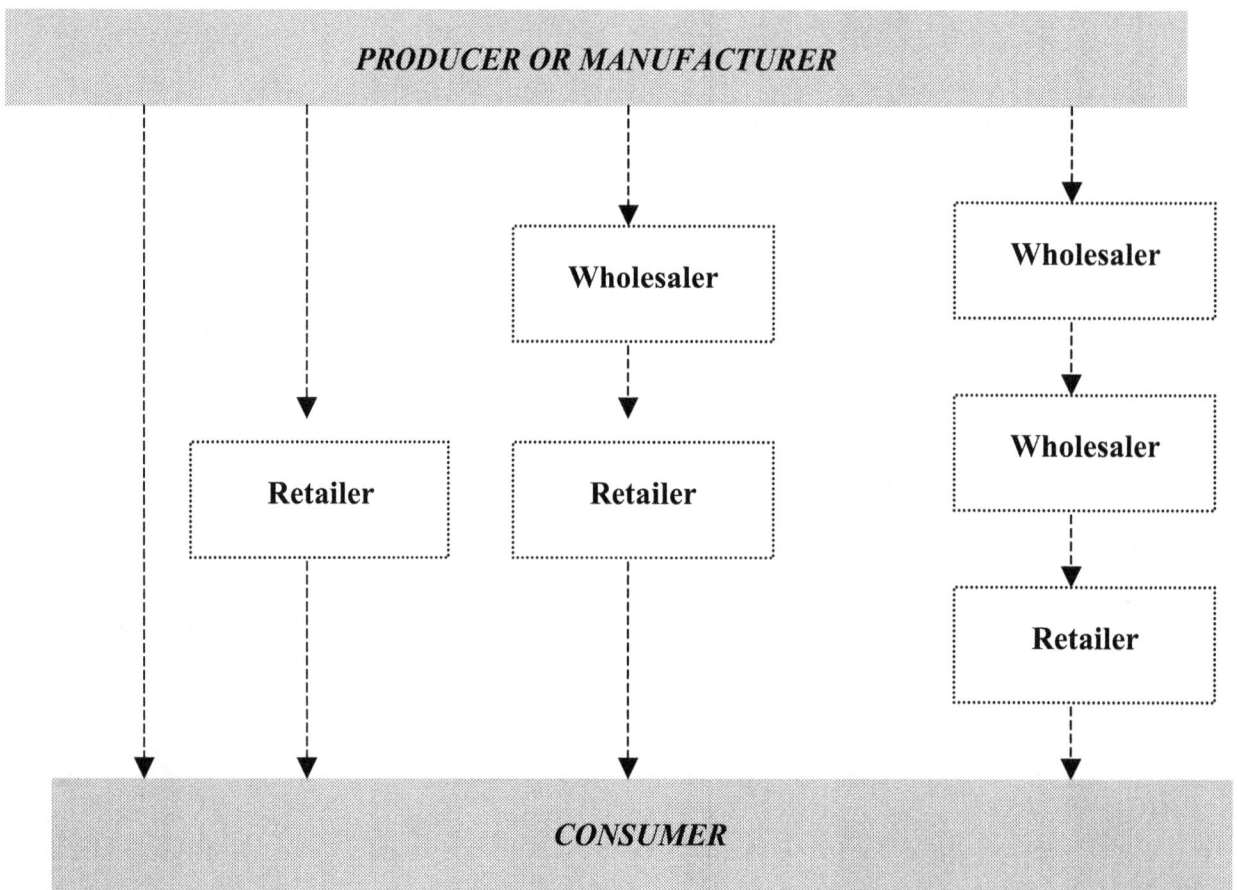

PRODUCER OR MANUFACTURER

```
                              Wholesaler              Wholesaler

                                                      Wholesaler
         Retailer             Retailer
                                                      Retailer
```

CONSUMER

Promotion

Promotion involves persuading the target market to purchase your product or service. Sales promotion can use either **direct** or **indirect** methods. **Direct** promotion methods include advertising, publicity, displays, special event sales, and personal selling; whereas, **indirect** promotion methods include public relations, customer relations, customer services, and product packaging. Another part of promotion is **advertising**. For the new firm, advertising is particularly important because new or potential customers must be made aware of the firm's existence. Even though word-of-mouth advertising is fine and, in fact, crucial, a firm cannot rely solely on this form of advertising. Small business people need to incorporate advertising costs into their budgets, allocating monthly amounts in this area. To be successful, advertising must be consistent, image building, and continuous. The new entrepreneur needs to start off with advertising which will bring immediate action (i.e., immediate response ads).

There are a variety of advertising media which can be used.

- Newspapers

- Magazines

- Radio

- Direct Mail

- Television

- Web Sites

- Point-of-Purchase Displays

- Bench Advertising

- Billboards

- Motion Advertising (public transportation)

- Fliers and Brochures

- Speciality Items or Novelty Items (such as pens, calendars, etc.)

- Free Publicity

- Telephone Yellow Pages

The selection of the best media for a small firm is not an easy endeavor. Television is not appropriate for most small firms due to the cost factor and the probability that you may be reaching many individuals who are not in your target market, thus incurring unnecessary costs. Large newspapers tend to be quite expensive. Local or community papers also tend to be somewhat expensive; however, local or community papers may be a viable option. Magazines, too, are somewhat costly, and with the exception of local magazines, may cover too much territory for a small business. Advertising spots on a local radio station may be feasible if the costs are in line and you can get the most advantageous time for reaching your target market.

Billboards often are effective near the location of the business but also are costly. Speciality advertisement, which includes calendars, rain scarves, and pens, tends to be effective and can be as costly or as inexpensive as you desire. Motion advertising may be effective if your market uses transportation such as buses, taxis, and subways on a routine basis. The telephone book should not be overlooked, as many potential customers do preshopping by the phone. Direct-mail advertising is used by a great number of small businesses. It is less expensive than many other forms of advertising and provides the small business owner with selective coverage. Your craft business should consider having a Web site which would detail all of your products and services. A Web site is really a "must have" in the 21st Century and should always be current. Never leave out-of-date information posted on your Web site. Under no circumstances, allow a telephone number to appear that is no longer a working number.

The goal of advertising is to sell by way of the **"AIDA"** formula. This formula means you must get the potential customers' **attention,** make them **interested** in your product or service, create a **desire** for your product, and bring about **action**--the purchase of your product or service.

Basic Advertising Guidelines

1. Start with the sales budget.

- Decide what percentage of your anticipated sales volume you will allocate to advertising. Use the following approach: research trade journals, estimate monthly sales, and consider special promotions.

2. Profile yourself and your customers.

- What business am I in?

- What quality of products do I sell?

- What kind of image do I want to project?

121

- How do I compare with the competition?

- What customer services do I offer?

- What are my customers' tastes?

- Why will they buy from me?

3. Select the appropriate advertising media for your business.

4. Adhere to the following pointers for printed ads.

- Make ads easy to recognize.

- Use simple layouts.

- Use dominant illustrations to feature services.

- Show the product's benefits to the reader.

- State a price or range of prices.

- Include the business name, address, phone number, e-mail address, and Web site.

- Repeat an ad if the response is good.

5. AIDA: Get the customers' **attention,** arouse their **interest**, make them **desire** your product   and finally, get them to take **action,** or buy your product. This is the goal of advertising.

<u>Measuring the Results of Advertising</u>

There are different types of advertisements and different measuring methods. **Immediate-response** advertising is designed to cause the potential customer to buy a particular product from you within a short time. The following is a list of tests to measure the response to the advertisements.

- Coupons brought in,

- Requests by phone or letters referring to the ad,

- Sales made of a particular service, and

- Business traffic

Attitude advertising is the reputation or image builder form of advertising. To measure its effectiveness:

- Run an ad every week and compare each week's sales with the same week of the previous year, and

- Ask customers how they heard about your business

Marketing Research

Marketing research is essentially a systematic way of finding general information that pertains to the marketing of one's own goods or services or learning about one's customers and/or competition. It assists one in determining who should be in the target market (group of people to whom you are addressing your efforts and trying to satisfy) and the demographic information and spending habits of those potential customers. In addition, it helps to verify whether you have the goods and/or services the customers want and whether the promotional strategy is appropriate and effective.

There are two major types of marketing research: **secondary** and **primary**. **Secondary** involves the utilization of published information, such as surveys, books, and magazines.

Primary research pertains to information obtained directly from one's target market. Primary research may take the form of a questionnaire (direct mail or personal), telephone surveys, test marketing, behavior observation, etc.

Marketing research does not have to be expensive because a great amount of the information can be gathered by the entrepreneur. License plates of cars in the parking area or neighborhood can provide an idea of where customers or potential customers live (county) so that advertising can be directed accordingly. Also, questionnaires can be utilized; and the examination of telephone numbers and zip code numbers given on a mailing list or personal check can provide an idea of the section of the city in which customers live. Coupons used in connection with radio ads that require customers to mention a radio station's name to get a special discount will also help to determine who is hearing certain ads. Of course, an observant entrepreneur is necessary. Looking at how customers dress, whether they are married and/or have children, and what age, ethnic background, likes, dislikes, and what other characteristics they possess is also important.

Using some form of marketing research, the potential entrepreneur needs to estimate the approximate size of the total potential market.

Attempt to estimate your market size. Indicate sources of data for your approximation. Some of the references from the bibliography should be helpful here. The approximate size of my market is _____.

It is also necessary to thoroughly analyze your competition. A table such as the one that follows may be helpful with this endeavor.

TABLE I

ANALYSIS OF COMPETITION

Name and Address of Competitor	% Estimated Market Share	Estimated Yearly Sales $	Comments on Competitor's Strengths and Weaknesses

How can you overcome your competitors' strengths to gain a competitive edge?

What market share (% of the market) do you think you can acquire?

Marketing Tactics

1. What methods will you use to sell your service (direct selling, Web site, yellow pages, radio ads, etc.)?

2. What are your long-range marketing plans?

3. Will you offer unique services and/or specialized care services?

4. How will you bring your service to the attention of potential customers?

5. What type of advertising will you use?

6. How much will it cost and how long will it take to establish a market share for your service? (Make a rough estimate.)

Examining the Economic Environment of Your Business

The total environment in which your business will be operating must also be considered when determining an appropriate marketing strategy. The North American Industry Classification System (NAICS) Code for craft and art businesses will vary, based on the total nature of the business; however, many are categorized under manufacturing. Please consult the NAICS Web site, www.census.gov/epcd/naics02, for details.

The following questions should be addressed.

1. How many firms are in this industry?

2. Do they vary in size?

3. Where are most of the enterprises located?

4. What is the relationship between small firms of this type and larger firms in the industry?

5. Do the firms serve English-speaking only or some bilingual markets?

6. What is the government's attitude toward this type of business?

7. What is society's attitude about your type of business or your industry?

8. What is the market for your business? Consider age, sex, education, birth rate, population trends, income, competition, etc. of your target market.

"When you are in business for yourself,

you have to learn to toot your own horn,

which is simply a dimension of marketing."

M.G.L.J.

CHAPTER V

FORMS OF BUSINESS OWNERSHIP

" Look into the future with vision and vivaciously

create a business climate based on values. "

M.G.L.J.

FORMS OF BUSINESS OWNERSHIP

There are three major legal forms of business ownership: the **sole proprietorship**, **partnership,** and **corporation**. One form cannot be said to be better than the other, as one must consider the advantages and disadvantages of each in light of his or her needs and desires. Below, the three forms are evaluated in terms of their advantages and disadvantages.

Proprietorship

An enterprise owned by one individual is a **proprietorship**. The owner and the business are one and the same and cannot be legally distinguished and separated in the eyes of the law. This is the most common form of legal ownership.

Advantages

- It is fairly easy to start.

- Legal assistance is not a necessity.

- The organizational structure is simple.

- The owner has freedom to make decisions and enjoy the profits.

- It is easy to dissolve.

Disadvantages

- The owner is liable for all the enterprise's debts.

- Liability is not limited to the amount of capital/total assets invested in the business. The owner's home, car, bank account, and other possessions may be claimed by people to whom he or she owes money.

- If the owner has personal debts, creditors can take assets of the business to satisfy demands.

- Sometimes it is difficult to obtain funding.

- Success is dependent on the owner's abilities.

- The legal life of the business terminates with the death of the owner.

Partnership

A **partnership** is the joining of two or more individuals to form an organization.

Advantages

- Gives you the opportunity to pool financial resources together.

- Provides the advantages of combining the additional skills and knowledge of partners. Allows the teaming of individuals who have complementary talent.

- Allows for division of labor and management responsibility.

Disadvantages

- General partners have unlimited liability.

- The death of a general partner terminates the partnership.

- General partners are responsible for the acts of each other partner.

- Partners cannot obtain bonding protection against the acts of other partners.

- There is the possibility of disagreement among partners.

There are two different types of partnerships:

1) **General** - Each partner is held liable for the acts of other partners.

2) **Limited** - This form can only be created by compliance with a state's statutory requirements. It is composed of one or more general partners. The liability of the limited partner is limited to the amount of funds he or she contributes.

A partnership should have an attorney draw up a partnership agreement. The partnership agreement usually includes sections addressing the following:

- name, purpose, and location

- duration of agreement

- type of partnership

- contribution by partners

- business expansion (how it will be handled)

- authority

- books, records, and the method of accounting

- division of profits and losses

- salaries

- rights of continuing partnership

- death of partner

- employee negotiations

- release of debts

133

- sale of partnership interests

- arbitration

- addition, alterations, and/or modification of partnership agreement

- settlement of disputes

- required and prohibited acts

- absence and disability

Corporation

A **corporation** is a legal entity which is separate and distinct from the individual. In the new or very small corporation, the stock in the corporation is described as "closed" or "closely held" and is not available to the general public in order for the owners to keep control.

Advantages

- The corporate form of ownership offers permanence--the business does not cease to exist if an owner dies.

- Owners of a corporation have limited liability (only the amount invested in the business).

- Corporations usually have greater borrowing power.

- Transferring ownership is relatively easy.

- Company expansion is relatively easy.

- In figuring the corporation's net income, salaries paid to employees and executives may be deducted as an expense item.

Disadvantages

- Incorporating can be costly and require detailed records which are often expensive and time consuming.

- Corporate income is taxed twice. First, the corporation pays tax on its income before it distributes dividends, and then shareholders pay taxes on dividends.

- The powers of the corporation are limited to those stated in the charter.

- The corporate form of ownership is more impersonal than the other forms.

S Corporations

The **S Corporation**, formerly known as the Subchapter S Corporation, is a form of organization which is specifically designed for closely held firms. The major difference between this type of corporation and regular corporations is the way in which they are taxed. In S Corporations, the profits are distributed to shareholders according to how much stock they own. The shareholders pay tax on the profits as personal income, with the corporation paying no tax as an entity. In essence, the stockholders are taxed as partners, thus avoiding the corporate income tax structure while allowing the firm to retain the limited liability feature of corporations.

S Corporations have many legal restrictions, including limitations to the number of stockholders, who may be stockholders, how profits are distributed, and the amount of fringe benefits allowed owner/employees.

You should consult your attorney and accountant to determine the advantages and disadvantages of this and other forms of ownership for your particular business. You should also consult your accountant about all tax considerations prior to actually implementing your business.

Limited Liability Company

The **Limited Liability Company (LLC)** is a hybrid between a partnership and a corporation in that it combines the "pass-through" treatment of a partnership with the limited liability accorded to corporate shareholders.

Advantages

- Historically, most states require that a Limited Liability Corporation (LLC) be comprised of at least two LLC members. Today, most states and the IRS recognize the single-member LLC as a legitimate business structure.

- Like limited partnerships and corporations, the Limited Liability Corporation shares a similar advantage--it is recognized as a separate legal entity from its "members."

- Most states require fewer formalities be observed in an LLC in comparison to a corporation.

- The LLC owner's liability is generally limited to the amount of money which the person has invested in the LLC. Thus, LLC members are offered the same limited liability protection as a corporation's shareholders.

- LLCs allow for pass-through taxation. This means that earnings of an LLC are taxed only once. The earnings of an LLC are treated like the earnings from a partnership, sole proprietorship, and most S corporations.

- Like general partnerships, LLCs are usually free to establish any organizational structure agreed on by the members. Thus, profit interests may be separated from voting interests.

Disadvantages

- Some states require that a LLC have more than one member

- Legal assistance is required to set up

- More paperwork is necessary than for an ordinary partnership

- Some states require that a dissolution date be listed in the articles of organization. This date may be amended. Further, certain events, such as death of a member, departure of a member, bankruptcy, etc. can be a dissolution event. A corporation has unlimited life, and these events are not dissolution events for a corporation.

- The LLC is a newer entity, and people are not as familiar with the LLC as a corporation.

The major legal considerations for a small business are as follows:

I. Choice of organizational form of ownership

    A. Proprietorship
    B. Partnership (general or limited)
    C. Corporation

II. Issues to address in organizational documents

    A. Procedures for voting
    B. Admission of new parties
    C. Providing continuity
    D. Resolving deadlocks
    E. Continuity in the event of death, disability, or bankruptcy of an owner
    F. Sources of capital

III. Business issues to consider in structuring a company

    A. Exposure to liability

        1. Product liability
        2. Environmental protection

3. Errors and omissions
4. Fraud allegations
5. Worker compensation
6. Defamation
7. Trademark and copyright infringement

B. Regulatory authorities

1. Licenses and permits
2. Securities regulation
3. Consumer protection
4. Labor relations
5. Environmental protection

IV. Registration with taxing authorities

A. Federal income taxes
B. Federal employment taxes and withholding
C. State employment taxes
D. Federal excise taxes
E. State sales and use taxes
F. State franchise and excise taxes
G. Miscellaneous state taxes
H. Local general property tax

Franchising

Franchising is a form of licensing by which the owner of a product, service, or process obtains distribution at the retail level through affiliated dealers. The owner of the product or service is called the **franchisor**. The affiliated dealer is known as the **franchisee**. Franchises are found in all industry areas, and being a franchisor may be a feasible option to consider in your plans for expansion and growth. Franchising is an option with many benefits. The benefits, however, vary from company to company.

Benefits

1. Franchising provides a chance to open a business without previous experience.

2. Franchising often provides a chance to open a business with less capital.

3. Many franchises provide financial assistance.

4. Franchises generally have a consumer-accepted image.

5. Franchises offer consistent quality.

o Franchising affords combined buying power, allowing for purchasing advantages.

7. Franchises offer basic training and continued assistance.

8. Franchises provide location analysis.

9. Franchising provides the financial capability to buy a choice location.

10. Franchising provides advantageous rental or leasing rates.

11. Franchisers assist in the development of well-designed facilities, fixtures and displays, and provide supplies.

12. Franchisers offer managerial and records assistance.

13. Franchisers offer sales, advertising, and marketing assistance.

14. Franchisers provide national publicity, promotion, and recognition.

15. Franchising affords higher income potential.

16. Franchises have a lower rate of failure.

17. Franchises provide continual research and development.

Disadvantages

Some of the disadvantages of franchising includes:

1. The subjugation of personal identity.

2. The submission to significant standardization and control.

3. The franchisee does not have the option of selecting unique services to offer.

Pointers for Evaluating a Franchise Opportunity

Before going into any franchise arrangement, the opportunity needs to be evaluated thoroughly. The following steps should be used when evaluating an opportunity:

➢ Check the opportunity out with the Better Business Bureau and Chamber of Commerce.

➢ Determine when the business was established.

➢ Determine what type of financing is provided.

➢ Ask the owners for a sample contract and study it with the advice of legal counsel.

➢ Determine if the company provides continual assistance.

➢ Find out how many of the franchises are now operating and where they are located.

➢ Determine what the failure rate for the franchises has been.

➢ Investigate how profits are running.

➢ Research the product's or service's quality.

➢ Evaluate the contract to be sure it covers all aspects of the agreement.

➢ Investigate what types of promotion will be provided.

Before any franchise agreement is signed, determine whether enough information about the proposed relationship has been obtained to understand fully the implications of the agreement. The following checklist may be useful in making that determination.[18]

Franchising Checklist

The Company

How long has the firm been in business?
Has it a reputation for honesty and fair dealing?
How does it rate with the Better Business Bureau?
Is the firm adequately financed so that it can carry out its stated plan of financial assistance and expansion?
Has the franchisor shown you any certified figures indicating exact net profits of one or more operating firms which you have checked personally?
How selective is it in choosing franchisees?
Has the franchisor investigated you carefully enough to assure itself that you can successfully operate one of its franchises?

The Product

What is the product's quality?
How well is it selling?
Have you conducted a study to determine whether the product or service which you propose to sell has a market in your territory at the prices you will have to charge?
Is the product priced competitively?
Is it packaged attractively?
How long has it been on the market?
Where else is it sold?
Will the product or service you are considering be in greater demand, about the same, or less demand five years from now?

The Sales Area

Is the territory well defined?
Is it large enough to offer good sales potential?
What are its growth possibilities?

Does the franchise give you exclusive territorial rights or can the franchisor sell a second or third franchise in your territory?

Is the franchisor connected in any way with any other franchise company offering similar merchandise or services?

If the answer is yes, what is your protection against this second franchisor organization?

What competition exists in your territory for the product or service you contemplate selling?

What is the territory's income level? Are there fluctuations in income?

Will the population in the territory increase, remain static, or decrease over the next five years?

The Contract

Does the contract cover all aspects of the agreement?

Does it benefit both parties?

Has your lawyer approved the franchise contract?

Does the franchise call upon you to take any steps which are, according to your lawyer, unwise or illegal in your state, county, or city?

Can the contract be renewed, terminated, or transferred?

Under what conditions will the franchise be lost?

What are the conditions for obtaining a license?

Under what circumstances and at what cost can you terminate the franchise contract?

If you sell your franchise, will you be compensated for your goodwill; or will the goodwill you have built into the business be lost by you?

Is a certain size and type of operation specified?

Is there an additional fixed payment each year?

Is there a percent of gross sales payment?

Must a certain amount of merchandise be purchased?

Is there an annual sales quota?

Can the franchisee return merchandise for credit?

Can the franchisee engage in other business activities?

Does the franchisor provide continuing assistance?

Will the firm assist you in finding a good location?

Is there training for franchisees and key employees?

Are manuals, sales kits, and/or accounting systems supplied?

Does the franchisor handle lease arrangements?

Does he or she design the store layout and displays?

Does he or she select opening inventory?

Does he or she provide inventory control methods?

Does he or she provide market surveys?

Does he or she help finance equipment?

Does he or she make direct loans to qualified individuals?

Does he or she actively promote the product or service?
How and where is the product being advertised?
What advertising aid does the franchisor provide?
What is the franchisee's share of advertising costs?
Exactly what can the franchisor do for you that you cannot do for yourself?

Questions Pertaining to Ownership

Answer the following questions to assess some of the key aspects of deciding what form of business organization is best for your firm.

What legal structure would insure the greatest adaptability for the administration of your firm?

What are the possibilities of attracting additional capital?

What are the needs for and possibilities of attracting additional expertise?

Which legal structure would best serve your purpose? Why?

"Formula for perpetual ignorance:

Think you know it all."

M.G.L.J.

CHAPTER VI

NEW
VERSUS
AN ESTABLISHED BUSINESS

" Successful entrepreneurs are intuitive,

display integrity in all of their actions,

and approach challenging situations with ingenuity."

M.G.L.J.

NEW BUSINESS VERSUS AN ESTABLISHED BUSINESS

The question may have already crossed your mind as to whether to buy a business that is already operating or to begin your own. Below are some considerations you should address when evaluating this question.

Just because a business is already established does not mean that success is guaranteed. The same very careful analysis that is conducted for a new enterprise must be done for an established business, including the consideration of target markets, location factors, and capital requirements.

Acquiring an Established Business

Both pros and cons must be considered when the entrepreneur is making the decision about the feasibility of acquiring an existing enterprise.

The Pros

1. The building, equipment, and people are already functioning.

2. The product is already being produced.

3. A market is established for the product or service.

4. Revenue is probably being generated.

5. The location may be desirable.

6. Financial relationships have been established.

7. Inventory is already in place.

8. Verifiable information about the business and industry can be obtained from the previous owner.

The Cons

1. The facilities may be old.

2. The personnel may be poor and inappropriate for the new owner.

3. Employee/management relations may be bad.

4. The inventory, if any, may be out-of-date and useless.

5. The location may be poor.

6. The financial condition may be poor.

7. The firm's bad reputation may be inherited.

8. Space may be too expensive.

9. Equipment may be obsolete.

10. You may not know the real reason why the previous owner is giving up the business.

11. Records may be misleading.

When taking over an established business, there are six factors which should be closely examined.

- The real reason why the business is being terminated.

- The company's past sales and profits.

- The operating costs of the business (the use of operating ratios given on page 150 can be quite beneficial here).

- The condition of equipment and inventory (Is it old, obsolete, and/or in need of repair?).

- The value and condition of tangible assets.

- The value of the business as compared to the price being asked.

How to Enter an Existing Business

Examine the condition of the business by addressing the following:

1. Are the physical facilities run down?

2. Does the inventory contain mostly dead stock?

3. Is the market for the firm's product declining?

4. Is the business solvent?

5. What are the intentions of the present owner (e.g., health, retirement, or competition)?

Business Evaluation Pointers

Useful ways of analysing an existing enterprise include the following options.

- Analyze accounting information, and do a physical inventory to determine the accuracy of recorded data.

- Determine whether the firm's cash position is high or low compared to the industry.

- Use financial ratios to determine the health of the firm. The following ratios are commonly used in the examination of the health of a firm.

Current Ratio: Current Assets
Current Liabilities

MEASURES SHORT-TERM SOLVENCY. SHOULD BE AROUND 2/1.

Quick Ratio: Current Assets - Inventory
Current Liabilities

SHOWS ABILITY TO PAY SHORT-TERM OBLIGATIONS WITHOUT HAVING
TO SELL INVENTORY.

Debt to Equity Ratio: Current Liabilities + Long-term Liabilities
Equity

Note: Owner's Equity = Assets - Liabilities

SHOWS FIRM'S OBLIGATIONS TO CREDITORS

- Determine the amount of debt and the terms of that debt.

- Determine the validity of the financial statements.

- Check the age of the accounts receivable.

- Check the cash flow.

- Appraise the pricing formula.

- Appraise operations, plant, and equipment.

- How effective are personnel?

- What is the quality of production?

- What is the physical condition of the plant? Is the layout appropriate for your needs?

- What are the age and condition of the equipment?

- Conduct a feasibility study.

Establishing a New Business

So, why start a business from the ground up? Consider the pros and cons.

The Pros

1. You can create the physical facilities you want.

2. All modern equipment can be utilized as opposed to inheriting outdated equipment, as may be the case when taking over an established business.

3. Modern processes and procedures can be implemented.

4. New inventory can be purchased.

5. New personnel can be hired.

6. You can design your own management system.

The Cons

1. There may be a problem of selecting the right business to start.

2. The business has unproven performance records in sales, reliability, service, and profits.

3. There are problems in finding a location, building, equipment, and personnel.

4. The owner must train a new work force.

5. There is no established service quality.

6. There will be problems at the start.

7. There may be problems with establishing an appropriate accounting system.

8. There will initially be "bugs" in the operations.

9. There may be problems with establishing a customer or client base.

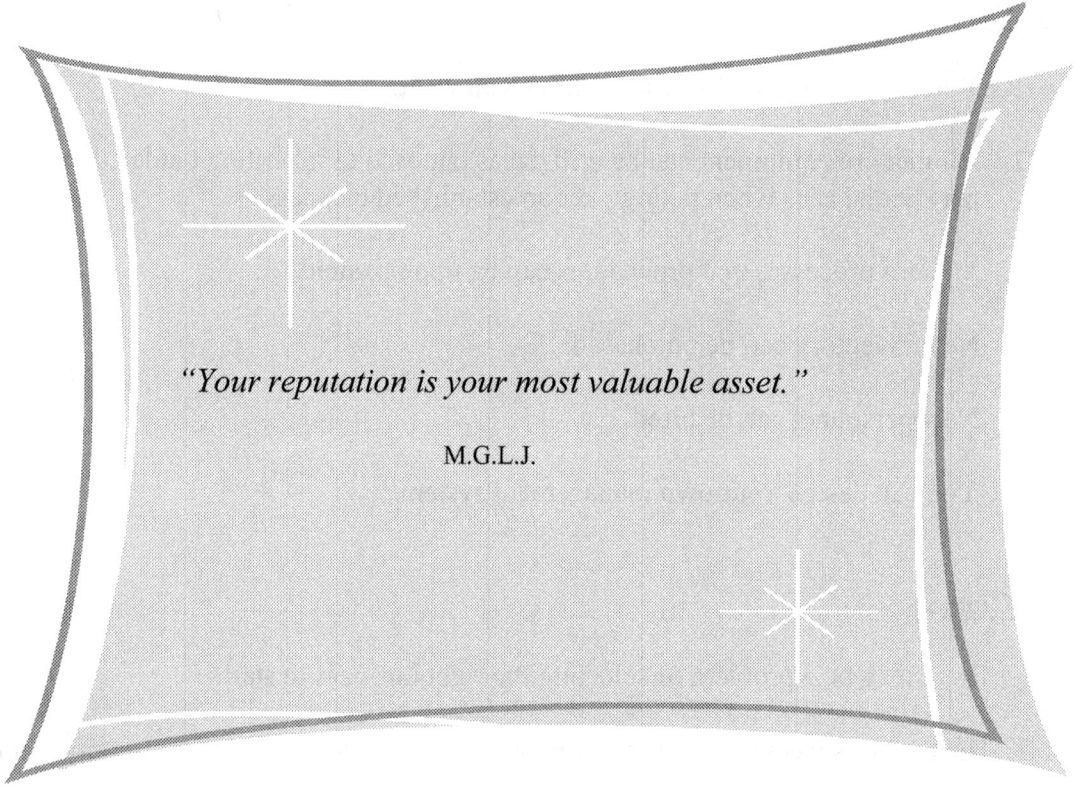

"Your reputation is your most valuable asset."

M.G.L.J.

CHAPTER VII

LOCATION

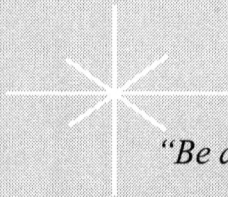
"Be deliberate in your actions

and move with determination and dignity."

M.G.L.J.

LOCATION

The importance of a good location should not be overlooked. Frequently, a prospective entrepreneur in search of a business home will take a location simply because a vacancy exists. Many factors need to be considered when examining a possible location.

Reaching Potential Customers

An overall assessment should be made of the city or town in which one wishes to locate to determine its receptiveness to her or his type of business. More specifically, one should examine the territory where he or she expects to find customers and determine if the specific site will serve the needs of the potential customers. The following questions should be considered:

1. Do the identified potential customers have the money to afford the services you will be offering?

2. What are the neighborhood service-use patterns?

3. Is transportation convenient to the business?

4. What are the traffic patterns and volume near the proposed business location?

5. Is there a good primary and secondary road access to the business?

6. Are there plans for new road construction or alteration of the present roads which may involve the disruption of traffic near the business and/or a bypass of the area?

7. Is there a good pool of qualified personnel available in the area?

Consider the enterprise location's proximity to major employers, public transportation, traffic arteries, etc. Further considerations are air quality and other environmental factors that impact outdoor activities (e.g., traffic, noise and volume, street safety, etc.).

Another factor to consider in site location is the proximity of competition. It is necessary to investigate the number of similar establishments competing for the same target market. Parking is a matter also deserving consideration. Ample parking is crucial in any business whose customers visit the business via car.

Of course, selecting a suitable building is also necessary; but this goes without saying and rests on good judgment as to the appropriateness of the facilities for the needs of the business. The following considerations should be ranked to serve as a guide in evaluating potential locations.

LOCATION CONSIDERATIONS

Grade each factor: "E" for excellent, "G" for good, "F" for fair, and "P" for poor.

Factor	*Grade*
Centrally located to reach your target market	
Supplies and equipment readily available	
Nearby competition situation	
Transportation availability and rates	
Quantity and quality of available employees	
Prevailing rates of employee pay	
Parking facilities	
Adequacy of utilities (sewer, water, power, gas)	
Traffic flow	
Crime/Safety factors	
Quality of police and fire protection	
Physical suitability of building	
Type and cost of lease or mortgage	
Provision for future expansion	
Other businesses promoting area	
Image of area as it relates to business image	
Zoning restrictions	

"You can always tell the pioneers

by the number of arrows in their backs."

M.G.L.J.

158

CHAPTER VIII

STAFFING

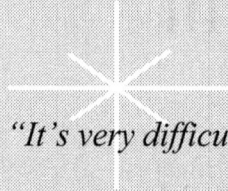

"It's very difficult to find good, capable, dependable,

honest employees. It's even harder to keep them.

Take time to praise and cherish your

most valuable resources."

M.G.L.J.

160

STAFFING

Good, dependable employees are crucial for business success. Hence, careful attention needs to be placed on acquiring appropriate, qualified, and reliable personnel. Policies must be developed for every aspect of your business, and personnel is no exception. You can determine your policies once you are in tune with your personality, your likes and dislikes, the objective and nature of your business, and situations that might arise. You also need to consider the different matters which might arise affecting employees and how you wish to handle them. Such policies are considered in the scope of the personnel function, which is wide and varied. It encompasses planning, selection and assignment of employees, performance appraisal, training, development, wage and salary administration, employee benefits, employee services, employee relations, communications, work environment concerns, union relations, reports and record keeping, and equal employment/affirmative action.

When examining specific employee needs, you must determine what jobs are really necessary to accomplish your objectives and then look at the specifics of the job to determine what type of qualifications a person should have for that position. After determining your specific personnel needs, there are different sources from which you can obtain employees, such as the state employment service, private personnel agencies, newspaper ads, and local schools and colleges. Touching base with organizations, associations and people in the community, as well as displaying a sign in your window, are all additional sources from which to obtain employees.

After deciding on the source or sources from which to obtain applicants, some form of screening process needs to be used so that the most appropriate person, based on the needs and desires of the firm, can be selected. It is necessary to develop a good application form in order to obtain all desired information, but make sure that questions are worded clearly and are in accordance with legal constraints (see next page for sample). References from applicants should also be requested. Applicants should, of course, be interviewed to find out as much as possible about each individual. The interview should involve asking specific, well-thought-out questions, the answers to which should give enough information about the interviewee to make the decision to hire or not to hire him or her. All applicants being considered for the job should be thoroughly evaluated in terms of the job interview and references before making the hiring decision. Remember, hiring the wrong employee can be very costly and even disastrous, so take time with the hiring process.

APPLICATION FOR EMPLOYMENT

Applicant's Name (Last)	(First)	(Middle Initial)	Social Security Number - -
Mailing Address (Number)	(Street)		Work Telephone Number ( )
City	State	Zip Code	Home Telephone Number
e-mail			( )

EDUCATION

Name of School	Location of School	Degree or Course of Study	Date Completed

Please indicate any special abilities, skills, training or relevant certifications that you feel particularly qualify you for the position.

EMPLOYMENT HISTORY – Begin with your most recent job. List each job separately.

Job Title	Dates Worked From To	Pay $ Per
Name of Employer	*Name of Supervisor*	
Address: City	State	Zip Code
Telephone Number ( )	Reason for Leaving:	
Duties Performed:		

Job Title	Dates Worked From To	Pay $ Per
Name of Employer	*Name of Supervisor*	
Address: City	State	Zip Code
Telephone Number ( )	Reason for Leaving:	
Duties Performed:		

Job Title	Dates Worked From To	Pay $ Per
Name of Employer	*Name of Supervisor*	
Address: City	State	Zip Code
Telephone Number ( )	Reason for Leaving:	
Duties Performed:		

May we contact the employers previously listed?   If not, indicate which ones you do not wish us to contact.

PERSONAL REFERENCES: List the names of three references whom we may contact.

1) Name	Telephone # ( )	Relationship (Teacher etc.)
Address: City	State	Zip Code
2) Name	Telephone # ( )	Relationship (Teacher etc.)
Address: City	State	Zip Code
3) Name	Telephone # ( )	Relationship (Teacher etc.)
Address: City	State	Zip Code

Training

The training aspect of personnel is an area often neglected in terms of importance. The success of a business rests heavily on having qualified, well-trained employees. The nature of training can take a variety of formats, such as on-the-job training, apprenticeships, internships, outside training, vestibule training, classroom training, and a myriad of combinations. Some outside training programs which may be of interest to the entrepreneur include the following:

- Manpower Development Training Act of 1962: Provides federal assistance in training unemployed and underemployed workers. The government reimburses you for part of the wages and training.

- Economic Opportunity Act (Anti-Poverty) of 1964: Firms hire individuals, and the government pays the cost of training.

- The JOBS Program (Job Opportunities in the Business Sector): You submit a proposal for contracts to provide on-the-job training for the disadvantaged employed, and you are paid additional costs incurred because of limited qualifications of those hired and trained.

- Training Programs offered by personnel development firms.

Employee Compensation

Employers must address the issue of the level of compensation for their employees. Factors generally considered are:

- Effort and time required for the job

- The entrepreneur's ability to pay

- Cost of living

- Government regulation

- Labor union considerations

- Supply and demand for workers, education level of employees, and industry and area rates

- Incentive plans

- Bonuses based on profit

- Pension plans

Employee Relations

The following guidelines can be used in handling employee grievances effectively:

1. Assure employees that complaining will not prejudice their relationship with their immediate superior.

2. Provide a clear way of presenting grievances.

3. Minimize red tape and time in processing grievances.

4. Provide a way for employees who cannot express themselves easily to present grievances.

All employees should receive a handbook containing major company policies and employee concern areas. A sample table of contents of a typical employee handbook appears on the next page.

EMPLOYEE HANDBOOK

A potential investor, as well as the originator of a business venture, will need to know the key personnel who will be carrying out the objectives of the business. It is necessary for the entrepreneur to pull together a dynamic management and work team who possess the appropriate and necessary skills and knowledge to make the business a success. A good business plan encompasses the resumes of all of the key individuals in charge of operating the business. On the following page you will find a suggested format for including information about all key personnel. Make sure that you capitalize on all skills, experience, and training that directly and indirectly relate to the nature of the proposed venture. Make sure that you have aligned yourself with the right combination of key persons. At this time, you may want to go back to Chapter I and reassess your skills, abilities, and personal characteristics. Make sure that you have personnel who can compensate for your weak areas and strengthen your stronger areas.

Address   **Phone, Fax, E-mail**

Name

Experience

(List your current or most recent job first; positions held and name of companies; work experience and knowledge in the field of the proposed venture)

Education

(Begin with highest level attained, including schools and year graduated or year training was completed; major and minor courses of study; significant school activities.)   Be certain to highlight training relevant to your proposed venture.

Special Skills and/or Certifications

(List all specialized training, skills, and relevant certifications)

Professional Affiliations

(List all professional organizations in which you hold membership)

Awards & Honors

(List all awards and honors)

Community and Civic Affiliations

(List all community involvement and volunteer service activities)

References

(List at least 3 good references, preferably individuals well known in the industry of your proposed business venture or well known in the community, nationally, or locally.)

ENTREPRENEURS

1. What key managerial skills and expertise does the proposed venture need to succeed?

2. Indicate the crucial specialists necessary to consult for success (attorneys, marketing people, accountants)

3. Indicate the primary individuals involved in your firm, including co-founders and their principal skills. Include your own skills and experience with this type of business.

4. List the type of personnel needed for the operation of your business. Include an employee handbook in this section, along with responsibilities of all personnel. (See example of Table of Contents.) All firms, regardless of size, should prepare an employee handbook which summarizes employee-concern areas and policies and serves as an easy reference for the employee as well as the employer.

"When we are foolish, we want to conquer the world.

When we are wise, we want to conquer ourselves."

M.G.L.J.

CHAPTER IX

ORGANIZING THE BUSINESS

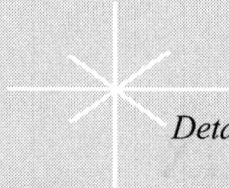

Details, Details, Details.

"Pay attention to the details even though it may seem

that you are spending too much time on them.

Excellence is in the details."

M.G.L.J.

ORGANIZING YOUR BUSINESS

Regardless of the size of your business venture, there is a need for some systematic way of doing things or some form of organization. A good way of approaching organizational structure is to consider all the activities necessary to accomplish the objectives of the firm. Categorize or put these activities into feasible divisions, and establish appropriate authority for each grouping. The entrepreneur must thoroughly define the personnel required for the accomplishment of the activities of each grouping, prepare an organizational chart, and then thoroughly re-examine all activities and groups for efficiency and effectiveness.

Such a procedure involves delegation of authority and responsibility. Delegation itself is often difficult for the entrepreneur because it involves letting loose of some of the decision making and control. Nevertheless, proper delegation of authority is necessary for success. One of the main keys to effective delegation is knowing what to delegate and having competent and reliable employees to whom to delegate. With the delegation of authority goes the assignment of responsibility for the completion of the delegated tasks. However, accountability cannot be delegated. The entrepreneur is responsible for the successful operation of the firm, and how successfully the delegated tasks are accomplished will still fall back on the business owner's shoulders. Consequently, the importance of competent employees is evident, along with the necessity for a formalized system of control.

Basic Organizing Principles

Two basic organizing principles that will help the entrepreneur to plan the successful operation of the enterprise are:

1. Unity of Command

Employees should have only one superior to whom they are directly responsible.

2. Parity of Authority

Authority should be equal with responsibility. When delegating responsibility, measures must be taken to make sure employees have enough authority to perform their duties and responsibilities, but not more authority than necessary. Be sure employees have a written statement of their duties, authority, responsibilities, and relationships.

Ways of Organizing Your Business

Seven common ways of structuring a business include organizing by the following:

1. **Function** - similar skills are grouped to form a functional unit

2. **Product** - the business is structured according to the individual goods or services offered to the public.

3. **Process** - similar processes, such as customer service or production, are the basis for organizing the firm.

4. **Geographic area** - some firms have locations in different geographical areas and are organized primarily on the basis of territorial concerns.

5. **Type of customers serviced** - some firms service different types of customers, such as wholesalers and retailers, and are structured accordingly.

6. **Project** - some firms, such as consulting businesses, are organized internally based on projects being researched or worked on.

7. **Individual talents of subordinates** - some organizations are structured based on the particular areas of employee expertise.

Following, you will find a simple organizational chart for a small artisan shop. This organizational structure shows an obvious, direct relationship between the owner and the customer served. With growth comes the need for a slightly more complex structure and the delegation of duties. The second chart illustrates growth in this firm. As the firm continues to grow, it will become necessary to employ more personnel and distribute more of the duties and responsibilities by creating new positions and/or departments.

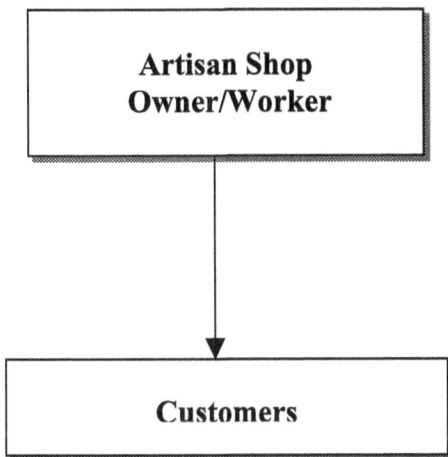

Artisan Shop Owner/Worker

↓

Customers

Artisan Shop Owner

↓

Artisan Shop Manager

↓   ↓

Worker		Worker

↓   ↓

Customers

Figure 1 One-Person Service

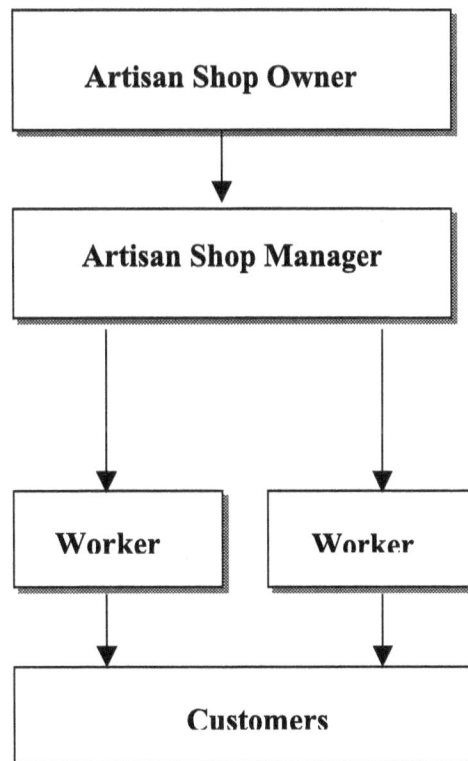

Figure 2 Expanded Service

"Entrepreneurs have to learn to delegate

and let some things go.

But don't lose sight of the fact that no one

will be as committed to your dream as you are.

So, keep your eye on your prize."

M.G.L.J.

CHAPTER X

FINANCING YOUR BUSINESS

"You will pass those who discouraged you

from pursuing your entrepreneurial dreams

on the stairway to success.

They will be sitting on the steps,

still passing out negative thoughts and going nowhere"

M.G.L.J.

FINANCING YOUR BUSINESS

If you are on a limited budget, a good initial strategy is to minimize your outlay on physical items and spend more on equipment, advertising, and your services. All businesses, regardless of the type, will need money to get started and to operate.

After you determine the size of your initial operations, you will have to follow an estimating process of the costs of these essential items and any others appropriate for your establishment. You will need to have enough cash to take care of your operational expenses for several months. Your capital, in essence, should provide enough to keep you going until you can start turning a profit.

The capital you need to be acquiring is often grouped into several categories:

1. Fixed capital: money for the building, equipment, fixtures, and vehicles.

2. Working capital: money for running the business on a day-to-day basis. This covers items such as utilities, money for buying inventory, insurance, advertising, salaries, rent, savings, cash, accounts receivable, etc.

3. Funds for personal living costs: capital to provide for you and your family until the business brings a profit.

4. Money cushion: extra money for unforeseen and unexpected costs.

It is crucial to have sufficient capital. The drawbacks of not having enough capital include:

- business failure

- inability to afford good employees

- investment in sub-standard or inadequate equipment

- inadequate inventory

- inability to obtain a good credit rating

- inability to obtain quantity discounts and other cost advantages

After thoroughly assessing your monetary requirements for starting and operating your venture, you will need to identify sources from which monies can be obtained for starting and operating your enterprise. There are many ways to obtain money to start and operate your business. Business financing is categorized as either **equity** or **debt financing**.

Equity financing represents money which the owner and/or others put into the business. All parties are at risk and at the same time stand to reap rewards. Equity financing is used for starting a business, expanding a business, and financing acquisitions. Equity financing includes personal savings and assets, money from family and friends, investments by key employees, and funds from venture capitalists.

Debt financing, on the other hand, is money loaned to businesses for a fee or interest. The funds borrowed, therefore, must be repaid. Debt financing is also used for business start up, operating funds, and expansion funds. Debt financing includes funds from commercial banks, savings and loans, savings bonds, commercial finance companies, small business investment corporations, federal programs, franchisers, or project organizers.

Sources for Financing Your Enterprise

There are many sources from which funds may be borrowed. They include the following:

Private Investors. Members of the family, friends, business associates, equipment dealers (if the equipment is bought on an installment basis or leased), and wholesalers of products (when they offer 30 to 90 days of credit before demanding payment).

Business Firms. Various business sources, such as:

- Banks

- Savings and loan companies which refinance home mortgages and make property-improvement loans

- Personal finance companies

- Finance companies which provide commercial credit (listed in the yellow pages and advertised in classified and financial sections of newspapers)

- Life insurance companies (some make loans to policy holders)

- Small business investment companies (these companies are licensed by the Small Business Administration to make long-term loans and guarantee bank loans, and they will provide equity financing by actually buying a share of the business)

- Development corporations which are formed by private citizens or businesses to promote the economy in their area

- Venture capital associations or groups of investors looking for businesses with promising futures (they usually provide equity financing, and they often advertise in the classified section of the newspaper want ads and via various Web site listings)

Federal Government. Some of the federal funding sources available are:

- Small Business Administration (SBA)

- Veterans Administration (VA)

Commercial Banks. One of the major sources of borrowing capital is a local commercial bank. It is crucial to have good rapport with your banker. Loans are generally either short-term or long-term in nature. Short-term generally represents money extended for a year or less, and long-term represents money extended for a period over a year. Loans are categorized as secured/collateral loans or unsecured. In the first type, the borrower is asked to pledge something such as life insurance, securities, equipment, real estate, or some other asset belonging to the loan seeker or the business. In the second instance, no security is required; and the loan is made based more on one's financial reputation, managerial ability, bank's evaluation of the business's soundness, etc. Your personal character, business reputation, adequate records, ability to repay the loan, and suitable collateral are all important necessities in obtaining a loan.

Personal Savings, Family and Friends. Your personal savings should be used as a last resort. If you obtain a loan from a bank, always spend the bank's money first.

Friends and family will frequently be receptive to lending you money, particularly if your business plan reflects significant research, and you can convince them that you can give them a greater return on their money than they would be able to obtain from a bank. Be sure when using this form of financing that you protect yourself with a buy-back contract or promissory note at the beginning of the financial relationship. The contract should make it worthwhile for your friends and family to invest in your business. At the same time, it should protect your ownership in the company when you become highly successful. Be cautious with family and friends' financial assistance. Personal relationships can become extremely strained when money is involved.

Life Insurance Policies. Individuals can borrow a major percentage of the cash value of their life insurance policies that have "paid-in" equity. These loan rates are generally much lower than bank loan rates. This form of financing should be investigated if you have such policies, but make sure you know any and all ramifications of borrowing on the equity.

Credit Cards. Credit cards are the most expensive way to finance your business due to the comparatively high interest rates. Try to avoid this form of financing.

Suppliers. Be familiar with all trade credit options. Creative terms with vendors can significantly affect your cash flow so that you have more money available when it is needed. Also, many suppliers, just for the asking, will pay you money if you are using their products. For example, a wholesaler or distributor of yarn may compensate you if you advertise that you are only using their unique yarn products.

Mortgaging Real Estate. Mortgages on residential property may sometimes be used to finance a business. You should contact your mortgage company for specific information about this form of financing. Be sure to assess the ramifications of using this type of financing, including the fact that you may lose your property if the loan is not repaid in a timely manner.

Savings and Loan Associations. Savings and loan associations historically have specialized in real estate financing, making loans on commercial, industrial, and residential properties. Savings and loan associations are now also beginning to offer the usual type of business loans available through commercial banks.

Venture Capitalists. Venture capitalists are affluent investors who need tax write-offs. They will invest money in your firm in return for your making them limited partners in your business. The majority of all new businesses have losses at first, and some wealthy investors are looking for losses to get tax breaks. You should obtain the assistance of an accountant and attorney before getting involved with venture capitalists.

Small Business Administration. The SBA defines a small business as one that is independently owned and operated and not dominant in its field. They have the specific objective of promoting the small business contribution to the nation's economic growth. By law, they are not allowed to make a loan if the funds can be obtained from a bank or other private source. Therefore, the first step is to try to obtain financing through regular channels. If the loan is turned down, then ask the bank to make the loan under SBA's Loan Guaranty Plan or participate with SBA in a loan. If the banker is interested, ask her or him to contact

184

the SBA to discuss your application. Usually the SBA will deal directly with the banker. The Small Business Administration will consider making a direct loan when these other forms of financing are not obtainable.

Summary of types of loans available from SBA:

1. Guarantee Loan: The SBA will guarantee up to a certain amount of money loaned to a small businessperson.

2. Participation Loan: SBA and the lending institution each put up part of the funds for the loan.

3. Economic Opportunity Loan: The SBA will lend money to any resident of the United States, Puerto Rico, or Guam if:

    a. Total family income from all sources (excluding welfare) is not sufficient for the basic needs of the family, and

    b. Due to social or economic disadvantages, the person has been denied the opportunity to acquire adequate financing through normal channels on reasonable terms. This includes honorably discharged Vietnam-era veterans.

4. Lease Guarantee Program: This is the issuance of an insurance policy or the reinsuring of a policy issued by a private insurance company which guarantees the rent for a small businessperson. A small business is often unable to lease a strategic location because it does not have a prime credit rating as required by some property owners. A guarantee that the rent will not be defaulted on is a valuable negotiating tool in locating a site.

5. Minority Loans: Loans are processed under somewhat relaxed criteria to encourage minority individuals to pursue business ownership.

The SBA also furnishes individual assistance to small businesspersons in the form of counseling, advice, and specific information of various types of business enterprises. The SBA requires all information and an assortment of papers that any other lender would. They will ask the same questions. They require collateral or some other guarantee of repayment, though good character and business ability may weigh more heavily with them than with a bank. However, they do state that the borrower should be able to provide sufficient funds from his or her own resources to have a reasonable amount at stake in the early stages of a new business. Certain SBA loan programs are phased in and others eliminated periodically, so check with your local SBA office for additional information.

Veterans Administration. The purpose of the VA program is to enable the veteran to obtain home, farm or business real estate, supplies and equipment, and working capital. The VA guarantees or insures various types of loans made by private lenders. If you qualify, then the various lenders (banks, savings and loans, etc.) would have to be contacted to determine if they make VA business loans and to set up an appointment. If a loan is not available in this way, the VA can make a direct loan in some cases.

Additional Ways of Obtaining Financing. Various other types of financing are as follows:

1. Financing by selling ownership of the business: Partnership arrangements, corporate arrangements, and public venture capitalists, or small business investment companies

(SBIC's) which are privately owned venture capital firms eligible for federal loans to invest in or lend to businesses.

2. Commercial Finance Companies: Firms which specialize in higher risk loans and generally charge higher interest rates than commercial banks.

3. Consumer Finance Companies: Financing arranged as a personal loan to one or several of the people in the business.

4. Trade Credit: Obtaining credit and financing from suppliers by their extension of terms of payment.

5. Factoring: This form of financing involves the outright sale of a business' accounts receivables to another firm, called a factor. The factor then pays cash to the business for its accounts receivables at a charge for each invoice plus interest on its advance.

Pointers for Successful Debt Financing

- If you are presently working, try to borrow funds while still employed. Studies show that banks are less likely to give you a loan when you do not have a "steady job."

- Make sure that you have devoted great attention to your marketing plan. Bankers want to know that there is actually a substantial market for your business and that you know how to capture the market successfully.

- Be able to sell yourself to the banker, and this includes looking like a businessperson.

- Try to search out a banker who is familiar with your industry.

- Fill out loan documents and applications neatly and accurately.

- Keep trade secrets to yourself. Do not share the details of your unique features unnecessarily. Share enough to establish the fact that you can obtain the competitive edge in the market, but the banker does not need to know everything.

- Under capitalization is a major cause of business failure. Make sure you have accurately assessed your start-up and working capital requirements for at least one year before you initiate your venture. Examine all of the financing sources mentioned in this chapter and determine what is right for you. A sample personal financial statement is included in the appendix to help you determine your personal net worth and assess what collateral you may have to help you find funding for your venture.

CHAPTER XI

BUSINESS RECORDS

"Tough times don't last, but tough women do."

M.G.L.J.

BUSINESS RECORDS

The novice entrepreneur probably would want to use the services of an accountant to set up the appropriate business accounting records. The following information is designed to provide you with some insight as to the types of records your accountant should establish, the purpose of each of these records, and the information they should provide you.

Before obtaining funds from whichever source is feasible, it is necessary to have accurate financial records and statements to present to your potential funder. These records are also necessary for successful business operations. Keeping accurate, concise, and appropriate business records is necessary for business success. A great majority of businesses that have failed did not keep accurate records. Good records show whether a business is making a profit, how much profit, and whether the business is efficient and growing. Good records also help you to identify specific problem areas.

For the purpose of efficient business operations as well as funding attainment, all businesses need the following basic financial records:

- **A Record of Cash and Record of Sales Receipts**

- **The Balance Sheet** lists the firm's assets and liabilities. It shows what the business is worth, what the owner owes, and what the obligations are. To be accurate, total assets must equal total liabilities plus owner's equity.

- **The Profit/Loss Statement**, which is often called the **Income Statement**, lists the total sales, cost of goods sold or services rendered, operating expenses, and taxes required in order to obtain a profit, usually for a period of a month. It may take different forms, but is generally a statement of the total amount of goods or services sold less all expenses and costs levied against sales to determine profit or loss from one's operations. Again, this is another statement which helps the entrepreneur determine the efficiency of the business operations and locate problem areas; and it addresses the question of whether or not a profit was made. The most common method of measuring profit is to find out what net profit is, and this is usually calculated on a monthly basis. Net profit is found by taking the total sales for the month and subtracting the cost of sales, which is the total of all expenditures that went directly into whatever was sold.

- **Accounts Payable Record** represents a list of one's suppliers and the amount owed to each.

- **Accounts Receivable Record** shows a list of what each credit customer owes you. It should also show what and when each customer purchases, and is a record of all payments received.

- **Cash Payments Journal** shows all expenditures, including date, expense identity, and reason,

- **Payroll Record** shows gross and net amounts of salaries paid, date of transactions, amount of taxes withheld, and holdings.

- **Schedule of Depreciation** calculates the decrease in value of equipment and furnishings so as to determine net worth. Depreciation schedules are basically lists of the major equipment and furnishings a company owns.

- **Withdrawal and Capital Record** shows what the owner puts in or takes out of the business and serves as a record of transactions which affect ownership.

Good records should show the financial status of the business, trends in the business, and provide important information about your business as well as point to problem areas. The following sample statements, presented in simple form, illustrate the usage of several basic records. The actual records and statements for an operating business, of course, will involve more detailed work than these three (3) statements; and again, it is recommended that the services of an experienced accountant be employed.

Elegant Art and Handcrafts
Income Statement
For Month Ended July 31, 20__

Sales		$ 30,000.00
Operating Expenses		
Salaries Expenses	$ 2,000.00	
Rent Expense	700.00	
Automobile Expense	400.00	
Supplies	100.00	
Miscellaneous Expenses	200.00	
Total Operating Expenses		3,400.00
Net Income		$26,600.00

This Income Statement shows the total sales for the month of July, which were $30,000, from which was subtracted the total expenses for that same period, $3,400, thereby providing the total net income for the month of July of $26,600.

Elegant Art and Handcrafts
Capital Statement
For Month Ended July 31, 20__

Capital, July 1, 20__		$10,000.00
Net Income for July	$26,600.00	
Less Withdrawals	2,000.00	
Increase in Capital		24,600.00
Capital, July 31, 20__		34,600.00

The Capital Statement shows the amount of capital the owner had in the business at the beginning of the time period, which was $10,000 on July 1. To this amount is added the net income for the month of July of $26,600 which can be determined by looking at your income statement, less withdrawals of $2,000 yielding an increase in capital of $24,600. The increase in capital for the month of July added to the beginning capital gives the total capital position at the end of the month of $34,600.

Elegant Art and Handcrafts
Balance Sheet
July 31, 20___

Assets

Cash	$18,600.00
Accounts Receivable	15,000.00
Supplies	3,000.00
Total Assets	36,600.00

Liabilities

Accounts Payable	$ 2,000.00

Capital

Elegant Expressions,Captital	$34,600.00
Total Liabilities & Capital	$36,600.00

The Balance Sheet visually depicts the accounting equation: **Assets = Liabilities + Owner's Equity.** This statement lists the firm's total assets as of July 31, which were $36,600, along with the total liabilities or total debt of the firm of $2,000, and the owner's capital of $34,600.

$$A = L + OE$$
Assets = Liabilities + Capital or Owner's Equity

$$\$36,600 = \$2,000 + \$34,600$$

A potential financier for a new business will be particularly interested in the following information and statements:

1. Start-Up Costs (Estimated)

2. Owner's Living Expenses (Estimated)

3. Operating Costs (Projected)

4. Balance Sheet (Projected)

5. Profit/Loss (Income) Statement (Projected)

6. Cash Flow Statement (Projected)

7. Break-Even Analysis

The small business owner on a daily basis should:

1. Check cash on hand.

2. Check the bank balance.

3. Check the daily summary of sales and cash receipts.

4. Make sure that all errors in recording collections on accounts are corrected.

5. Make sure that a record of all monies paid out, by cash or check, is maintained.

The small business owner on a weekly basis should:

1. Check accounts receivable, and take action on delinquent accounts.

2. Check accounts payable, and take advantage of discounts for early payment.

3. Make sure payroll records are in order.

4. Make sure taxes and reports to State and Federal Government are prepared and sent.

The small business owner on a monthly basis should:

1. Make sure that all Journal entries are posted to the General Ledger.

2. Assess the Profit/Loss Statement.

3. Assess the Balance Sheet.

4. Make sure the Bank Statement is reconciled.

5. Make sure the Petty Cash Account is in balance.

6. Make sure that all Federal Tax Deposits are made and that Withheld Income and FICA Taxes (Form 501) and State Taxes are paid.

7. Make sure that Accounts Receivable are aged, i.e., 30, 60, 90 days, etc., and collect past dues.

8. Check inventory.

"It's not the one who falls that fails,

but the one who falls, gives up, and never gets up."

M.G.L.J.

CHAPTER XII

SALES FORECASTING

"Never avoid the numbers.

They are the thermometer indicating the health

and wealth of your business."

M.G.L.J.

200

SALES FORECASTING

Once the decision has been made to go into business and the type of business has been selected, the next step is to forecast sales of goods or services for at least the first year. This is not an easy task, as you are dealing with many unknown factors; nevertheless, it is necessary to attempt to make an intelligent forecast using sound rationale. Sales forecasting requires you to predict the future as accurately as possible with justification for the forecasted figures. A forecast can be based on your personal judgment, interviews with people operating similar businesses, various types of published data, information from experts, as well as market calculations. Factors to take into consideration when forecasting sales include industry trends for your area; forecasts for retail craft businesses in your state, city, and area; and an assessment of your competition.

One approach to developing a sales forecast begins by estimating the total number of persons in the selected target market. This estimate comes from an analysis of your market via a survey and also from secondary sources such as **Statistical Abstracts of the U. S.**, marketing and demographic informational sources, and industry publications.

The following four equations will allow you to forecast sales:

(1) T x A = TPM

(2) TPM x P = TAM

(3) TAM x EMS = Sales in Units

(4) Sales in Units x PR = Sales in Dollars

201

Explanation:

(1) T x A = TPM

Total number of people in the target market multiplied by the annual number of purchases per person = total potential market.

(2) TPM x P = TAM

Total potential market multiplied by the percent of the total market coverage you think you might be able to obtain = total available market.

(3) TAM x EMS = Sales in Units

Total available market multiplied by the expected market share you expect to obtain = sales forecast in units.

(4) Sales in Units x PR = Sales in Dollars

Sales forecast in units multiplied by the price per unit = sales forecast in dollars.

When determining your expected market share, be sure to take into consideration the present market share of your competitors, the amount of promotion you will be using compared to your competition, the sales trends of similar services, and what the present competition may do to improve their present service when you enter the market.

CHAPTER XIII

THE INVESTMENT PROSPECTUS

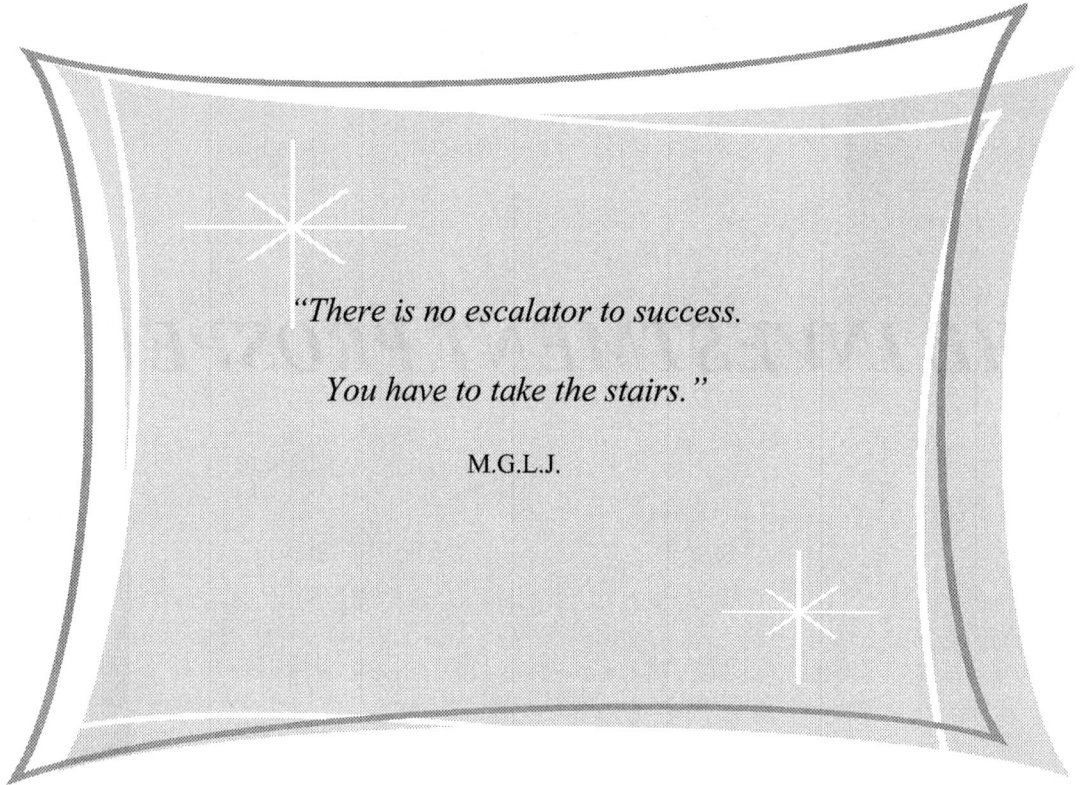

"There is no escalator to success.

You have to take the stairs."

M.G.L.J.

THE INVESTMENT PROSPECTUS

All important information about your business can strategically and, for impact purposes, be summarized in an investment prospectus. Someone considering investing in your business or lending you money wants to know exactly and quickly how much money you need and why they should lend it to you. (How profitable is it going to be?) Profit is important to an investor; however, many individuals considering venture initiation get entwined in the development of their idea into a business and fail to look at how profitable it stands to be. An outline of an investment prospectus follows.

Investment Prospectus Outline

Cover letter describing:
    Nature of business
    Amount of financing needed
    Terms of loan

Business description:
    Name and location
    Nature of business
    Organizational structure
    Product or service description
    Business goals
    Summary of financial needs and proposed use of funds

Market strategy:
    Market analysis
    Target market
    Competition
    Marketing objectives
    Price policies
    Distribution system
    Promotion

Production:
    Suppliers
    Production methods

Product services
Patents, legal, and technical information

Management:
  Management/ownership structure
  Education and work experience of board of directors and key personnel
  Personnel plan
  Compensation policy

Financial data:
  Financial statements
  Profit and loss statements (monthly for one year with explanation of projections)
  Balance sheets (projected one year after loan or investment with explanation of projections)
  Cash flow projection (monthly for one year with explanation of projections)
  Specific uses of investment funds
  Credit references

CHAPTER XIV

IS IT FEASIBLE?

"If the word QUIT is part of your vocabulary,

then the word FINISH likely is not."

Anonymous

IS IT FEASIBLE?

Your final considerations should address whether or not your proposed venture is feasible. Be sure you reiterate all significant justifications in this section.

The SBA provides a convenient checklist for those going into business. The following checklist affords a good opportunity to go back and make sure you have considered all necessary factors. Answer each question with a yes/no response. Then go back and evaluate your responses throughout the entire publication and determine if your proposed business venture is feasible and has a significant chance for success.

YOU

Are you the kind of person who can get a business started and make it go?

- ❏ Think about why you want to own your own business. Do you want a business badly enough to work long hours without knowing how much money you will earn?

- ❏ Have you worked in a business like the one you want to start?

- ❏ Have you worked for someone else as a supervisor or manager?

- ❏ Have you had any business training in school?

- ❏ Have you saved any money?

MONEY

- ❏ Do you know how much money you will need to get your business started?

- ❏ Have you counted how much of your own money you can put into the business?

- ❏ Do you know how much credit you can get from your suppliers?

- ❏ Do you know where you can borrow the rest of the money for your business?

209

- ❑ Have you figured out what net income per year you can expect to get from the business? Count your salary and your profit on the money you put into the business.

- ❑ Can you live on less than that amount so that you can use some of it to help your business grow?

- ❑ Have you talked with a banker about your plans?

FORM OF BUSINESS

- ❑ If you need a partner with money or know-how that you do not have, do you know someone appropriate and who is someone you can get along with and trust?

- ❑ Do you know the good and bad points about going into business alone, having a partner, and incorporating your business?

- ❑ Have you talked with a lawyer and an accountant about the appropriate form of ownership?

CUSTOMERS OR CLIENTS

- ❑ Do most businesses in your community seem to be doing well?

- ❑ Have you tried to find out whether enterprises like the one you want to open are doing well in your community and in the rest of the country?

- ❑ Do you know what kind of people will want to buy what you plan to sell?

- ❑ Do people who would want your product live in the area where you want to open your business?

- ❑ Do they need a business like yours?

- ❑ If not, have you thought about opening a different kind of enterprise or going to another neighborhood?

YOUR BUILDING

- ❑ Have you found a good building for your business?

- ❑ Will you have enough room when your business gets bigger?

- ❑ Can you fix the building the way you want it without spending too much money?

- ❑ Can people get to it easily from parking spaces, bus stops, or their homes?

- ❑ Have you had a lawyer check the lease and zoning restrictions?

EQUIPMENT AND SUPPLIES

- ❑ Do you know just what equipment and supplies you need and where they can be obtained from dependable suppliers?

YOUR SERVICE

- ❑ Have you decided what products you will sell?

- ❑ Have you found suppliers who will sell you what you need at a good price?

- ❑ Have you compared the prices and credit terms of different suppliers?

YOUR RECORDS

- ❑ Have you planned a system of records that will keep track of your income and expenses, what you owe other people, and what other people owe you?

- ❑ Have you worked out a way to keep track of your supply inventory so that you will always have enough on hand?

- ❑ Have you figured out how to keep your payroll records and handle tax reports and payments?

- ❑ Do you know what financial statements you should prepare?

- ❑ Do you know how to use these financial statements?

□ Do you know an accountant who will help you with your records and financial statements?

YOUR BUSINESS AND THE LAW

□ Do you know what licenses and permits you need?

□ Do you know what business laws you have to obey?

□ Do you know a lawyer you can go to for advice and for help with legal papers?

PROTECTING YOUR BUSINESS

□ Have you made plans for protecting your business against thefts of all kinds-- shoplifting, robbery, burglary, employee theft?

□ Have you talked with an insurance agent about what kinds of insurance you need?

BUYING A BUSINESS SOMEONE ELSE HAS STARTED

□ Have you made a list of what you like and do not like about buying a business someone else has started?

□ Are you sure you know the real reason why the owner wants to sell the business?

□ Have you compared the cost of buying the business with the cost of starting a new firm?

□ Are the supplies and inventory and building in good condition?

□ Will the owner of the building transfer the lease to you?

□ Have you talked with other businesspersons in the area to see what they think of the business?

□ Have you talked with the company's suppliers?

□ Have you talked with a lawyer about your proposed enterprise?

CHAPTER XV

CONCLUSION

"Never give up on your dream

just because it's taking too long for it to become a reality.

The time will pass anyway,

so you might as well be working on realizing your dream."

M.G.L.J.

MAKING IT GO

Consider the following questions as you refine your entrepreneurial vision.

ADVERTISING

- ❑ Have you decided how you will advertise? (Newspapers, Web site, posters, handbills, radio, direct mail, etc.)

- ❑ Do you know where to get help with your ads?

- ❑ Have you watched what other businesses similar to yours do to get people to buy?

PRICING

- ❑ Do you know how to figure what you should charge for each product you sell?

- ❑ Do you know what other enterprises like yours charge?

BUYING

- ❑ Do you have a plan for finding out what your customers want?

- ❑ Will your plan for keeping track of your inventory tell you when it is time to order more and how much to order?

- ❑ Do you plan to fill most of your needs from a few suppliers rather than a little from many, so that those you buy from will want to help you succeed?

SELLING

- ❑ Do you know how to get customers to buy?

- ❑ Have you thought about why you like to buy from some sales representatives while others turn you off?

YOUR EMPLOYEES

- ❑ If you need to hire someone to help you, do you know where to look?

- ❑ Do you know what kind of person you need?

- ❑ Do you know how much to pay?

- ❑ Do you have a plan for training your employees?

CREDIT POLICY

- ❑ Have you decided whether to let your customers buy on credit?

- ❑ Do you know the advantages and disadvantages of joining a credit card plan?

- ❑ Can you tell a deadbeat from a good credit customer?

A FEW EXTRA QUESTIONS

- ❑ Have you figured out whether you could make more money working for someone else?

- ❑ Does your family support your plan to start a business of your own?

- ❑ Do you know where to find out about new ideas and new services?

- ❑ Do you have a work plan for yourself and your employees?[19]

- ❑ Have you considered business regulations and insurance? Please reflect on the following.

REGULATIONS

Every potential business owner must become familiar with the different business regulations and laws affecting her or his type of business and, specifically, her or his area as they vary from locality to locality. These laws change from time to time so that it is necessary to obtain current information for your locality. The licenses and permits required to start a business vary among cities, counties, and states. The individual considering entrepreneurship should consult local government agencies or the local Chamber of Commerce for this type of information.

INSURANCE

Many businesses fail each year due to natural disasters, fire, damage suits, burglary, death of a partner, vandalism, employee theft, fraud, etc. Different types of insurance exist which can cover all of these different situations to minimize your risk. It is best to contact a reputable insurance company for your particular needs. Five kinds of insurance are essential: fire insurance, liability insurance, automobile insurance, workers' compensation, and crime insurance. Based on your particular business, you may need many additional types of insurance coverage. A good insurance company will be able to advise you about appropriate coverage. Also, consult a good attorney for advice on the appropriate insurance coverage for your business.

The operation of the proposed venture must be examined to determine if the sale of the product or service at certain cost levels seems feasible. The following concerns should be evaluated:

1. What are the major difficulties in the sale of the product or delivery of the service being considered?

2. Why do you think you can sell the venture's product or operate your service at competitive cost level?

3. Discuss the layout of your firm in terms of physical facilities.

4. Thoroughly consider and discuss all major risks and problems and address the minimization of the serious risks.

If you decide that your business is feasible, additional steps need to be taken in order to officially begin operations.

You should.....

- Obtain a business license from the city and/or county clerk.

- Obtain an employee federal identification number from the nearest Internal Revenue Service Office.

- Obtain an application for a sales and use tax certificate of registration.

- Comply with appropriate local, state, and federal regulations.

- Determine workers' compensation insurance requirements. State laws require employers to cover employees with workers' compensation insurance. Contact the State Department of Labor and obtain the form "First Report of Work Insurance" to determine your state requirements.

- Comply with the requirements of your State Division of Occupational and Health Association even if you employ only one person.

- Determine if certification by an appropriate board is required for your business.

- Contact your State Regulatory Board for necessary details.

- Check into local permits and ordinances.

- Check with your local or state Small Business Office or local Small Business Development Center to make sure you are in compliance with the regulations for your state and local municipality.

POINTERS FOR BUSINESS SUCCESS

This writer would like to close this publication with a few last pointers for small business success.

1. Develop a "total product" desired by the appropriate target market.

2. Please your customers.

   - Learn their likes and dislikes and make them feel that you are interested.

   - Given an extra bit of service, people will tell others.

   - It is the little things that count and that give your clients or customers that "warm and fuzzy" feeling and keeps them coming back.

   - Tell the truth about your service even if it means losing a sale. Telling the truth will make "would be" customers feel that you are an honest businessperson, and they will perhaps patronize you later or tell others.

   - Build a positive image.

   - Use a steady promotion plan and be consistent in everything you do.

3. Encourage teamwork.

   - Make employees feel that they are important to your business.

   - Praise employees in public; correct them in private.

   - Send your staff to workshops and seminars periodically. The knowledge obtained will allow them to benefit your organization more; and at the same time, it will elevate their feeling of worth to you and your organization.

4. Plan ahead.

5. Keep expenses in line and make a profit. Determine your break-even point.

6. Be involved in civic and community affairs. This is free advertising. Do benevolent

community deeds which will bring a positive image to your firm.

7. Keep your firm's name in the public's eye.

   - Always carry your business cards and brochures.

   - Have your business checks imprinted with your logo and a descriptive statement about your business. Checks pass through the hands of many individuals who may be in your target market.

8. Interact and socialize with people who can help you with your business concerns. "It's not what you know; it's who you know." This is an old cliche, but it is quite true in the world of small business. Particularly get to know a banker, lawyer, accountant, marketing/promotion specialist, local politicians, news media representatives, leaders of business, civic, service, political, educational, religious, and professional organizations, and the decision makers of the companies with whom you do business. You may also want to consider joining your local Chamber of Commerce.

9. Establish yourself as an authority in your field or industry. Use your contacts and get on the guest lecture circuit, talk shows, and community programs. You may even want to teach a class in your field as a part of the continuing education program of a local college. You may have to offer your teaching free initially, but the benefits derived will be great.

10. Establish credibility for your business.

11. Provide a good service at an acceptable price and back up your product with guarantees and warranties.

12. Live up to the commitments you make. Always deliver more than you promise; never promise more than you deliver.

13. Surround yourself with people who know more than you do. Hire staff personnel whose areas of expertise will enable you to expand your knowledge as well as expand your business.

14. Establish and maintain good credit.

15. Pay your bills on time. If you can't pay on time, call your creditor and see what other arrangements can be made. (These bills will not disappear, so face up to the problem which is quite common for small businesses.)

16. Take advantage of early payment discounts and quantity discounts whenever possible.

17. Always represent your business in a very professional manner.

- You are your business, and people will evaluate your business based on you. Your personal appearance is very important at all times, even on Saturday morning in the grocery store.

- Always wear clothes that are appropriate for your business field and that make you feel that you look good. You feel and act like you look.

- When greeting people, always use a firm, confident handshake with direct eye contact and a friendly smile.

18. Keeping cash flow concerns in mind, establish a feasible credit policy for customers and clients.

CHAPTER XVI

BUSINESS GLOSSARY

"Keep your eye on the prize--your entrepreneurial dream.

There are very few joys as wonderful as the joy of loving

what you do every day and getting paid for it."

M.G.L.J.

224

BUSINESS GLOSSARY

ANGELS	People who may be willing to supply capital to an entrepreneur with no strings attached. These individuals may include relatives, friends, or a mentor.
ASSET	An item of value owned by a business or individual.
BALANCE SHEET	A financial statement which lists the firm's assets and liabilities. It shows what the business is worth.
BALLOON PAYMENT	A final payment, generally on an installment loan, that is larger than the preceding payment.
BANKRUPT	The state of a person or firm unable to pay creditors and judged legally insolvent.
BOND	A long-term instrument used to finance the capital needs of a business or government unit.
BREAK-EVEN POINT	The volume of sales at which the firm's costs equal its income. Above the break-even point, a firm is making money. Below the break-even point, a firm is losing money.
BROKER	An agent who negotiates contracts of purchase or sale but does not take control of the goods.
BUDGET	An itemized summary of probable expenditures and income for a given period of time with a plan for meeting expenses.
BUSINESS PLAN	Document prepared by the business owners which details specific information about the firm.
BUYER	The person who makes the purchase decisions for a firm.

COLLATERAL	Property, stocks, bonds, savings accounts, life insurance, and current business assets which may be held to insure repayment of a loan.
CAPITAL	Cash or cash equivalents necessary to fund a business entity.
CAPITAL ASSET	An asset with a life of more than one year that is not bought and sold in the ordinary course of business activity.
CAPITAL BUDGETING	The process of planning expenditures on assets whose returns are expected to extend beyond one year.
CAPITAL GAINS (LOSSES)	Profits (or losses) on the sale of capital assets owned for six months or more.
CASH FLOW	A financial projection utilized by business owner(s) to evaluate receipts and disbursements over time. A cash forecast is used to predict high and low points in regard to profitability.
CASH FLOW PROJECTION	Forecast of the cash a business anticipates receiving and distributing during the course of a given span of time.
CASH MANAGEMENT	The practice of using the firm's money to earn money rather than allowing it to remain in accounts which do not pay interest.
COMMERCIAL BANK	An ordinary bank of deposit and discount, with checking accounts, as distinguished from a savings bank.
COMMON STOCK	The ownership element of a corporation represented by shares of stock.
COMPETITIVE EDGE	A particular characteristic (or characteristics) which makes a firm and/or product more attractive to customers than its competitors.

CONSIGNMENT	Goods placed by the supplier in the inventory of the consignee. The consignee pays the supplier only when goods are sold.
CONSUMER GOODS	Goods which are bought by the final user.
CONSUMER PRODUCT SAFETY COMMISSION	A federal commission with responsibility for establishing product safety standards and for taking appropriate steps to reduce unreasonable risks of injury or harm to consumers.
CONTINGENCY FUND	Monies set aside for unexpected expenditures.
CORPORATION	A form of business ownership which is considered a legal entity separate and distinct from the owner.
COST-BENEFIT ANALYSIS	An analytic technique of weighing the costs of a project or investment against the benefits derived from it.
COTTAGE INDUSTRY	Another term for the home-based business industry.
CPA	Certified Public Accountant.
CREDIT POLICIES	The firm's customer-payment policies.
DEBT CAPITAL	Monies loaned to the business owner which are used to increase and enhance the value of the firm. The money plus interest must be repaid over time and represents a debt for the firm.
DEBT FINANCING	Funds borrowed for certain business purposes and which must be repaid by the business to the lender.
DECENTRALIZATION	The degree to which decision making has been delegated downward in the organization.

DISPOSABLE INCOME	Personal income remaining after the deduction of taxes on personal income and other compulsory payments.
DROP SHIPMENT	The delivery of goods directly from a producer or wholesaler to the consumer.
DUN & BRADSTREET	A mercantile agency which offers credit ratings, financial analysis, and other financial services, usually on a contractual basis.
EBIT	Earnings before interest and taxes.
EMPLOYEE TURNOVER	The rate at which employees are hired and terminated or leave the organization.
ENTREPRENEUR	A person who organizes, manages, and initiates a business venture.
EQUITY	The net worth of a business which consists of capital stocks, capital (or paid-in) surplus, earned surplus (or retained earnings), and, sometimes, certain net worth reserves.
EQUITY CAPITAL	Money obtained by selling a part of the interest in the business.
FRANCHISOR	The owner of the product or service in a franchising relationship.
FRANCHISEE	The affiliated dealer through which a franchisor distributes products or services.
FRANCHISING	A form of licensing by which the owner of a product, service, or process obtains distribution at the retail level through affiliated dealers.
FIXED ASSETS	Assets of a business which are relatively permanent and are necessary for the functioning of the firm. Fixed assets include buildings, furniture, equipment, etc.

FIXED COSTS	Costs which remain constant regardless of changes in output. Fixed costs include interest on long-term loans, rents, salaries, etc.
FOB (FREE ON BOARD)	The point at which the title of goods transfers (free on board) from the producer to the buyer. FOB origin means that the title is transferred upon leaving the loading dock of the producer and that the shipping costs are paid by the buyer.
GENERAL PARTNERSHIP	A partnership arrangement in which each partner is held liable for the acts of other partners.
GOOD FAITH	A sincere belief that the accomplishment intended is not unlawful or harmful to another.
GOODS-IN-PROCESS	Goods in the midst of production or manufacture such that they are neither in a raw material state nor finished.
GOODWILL	Intangible asset based on the good image of a firm and established by the excess of the price paid for the going concern over its book value.
GROSS INCOME	Amount received by the firm before deducting operating expenses.
HOME-BASED BUSINESS	A business primarily operating out of the owner's or owners' home(s).
IMPULSE GOODS	Goods bought by consumers on sight to satisfy a desire that is strongly felt at the moment.
INVENTORY	The total of items of tangible property which a firm uses up or sells during a short time, including goods, material, supplies, and tools.
INVESTMENT PROSPECTUS	A document that highlights the major information regarding a business. This document summarizes information so that potential investors can quickly and easily evaluate a business venture.

INVESTMENT TAX CREDIT	A credit from federal income taxes that is computed as a percentage of the initial cost of certain capital assets.
JOBBER	A wholesaler or distributor.
LIABILITY	A debt or obligation of a business.
LIMITED PARTNER	The liability of the limited partner is limited to the amount he or she contributes to the enterprise owned.
LIMITED PARTNERSHIP	A partnership arrangement which is created by compliance with a state's statutory requirements. It is composed of one or more persons. One partner must be a general partner who has unlimited liability.
LINE AND STAFF	A descriptive term which defines the structure of an organization. Line refers to jobs or roles which have direct authority and responsibility for output. Staff personnel contribute indirectly or support line personnel.
LINE OF CREDIT	An arrangement whereby a financial institution commits itself to lend to a firm or individual up to a specified maximum amount of funds during a specified period.
LIQUIDATION	The process of terminating a firm's existence by selling its assets and paying its debts.
LIQUIDITY	A firm's cash position and its ability to meet maturing obligations.
LOSS LEADER	A product priced at a loss or no profit for the purpose of attracting patronage to a store.

MBO (MANAGEMENT BY OBJECTIVES)	A management technique of defining attainable goals for subordinates through an agreement of the supervisor and subordinates. It offers continual feedback to subordinates in terms of their contribution to the organization's total performance.
MANUFACTURER'S AGENT	An agent who generally operates on an extended contractual basis, often sells a definite portion of the principal's output within an exclusive territory, handles noncompeting but related lines of goods, and possesses limited authority with regard to prices and terms of sales.
MARKDOWN	A reduction in selling price. (An item priced at $1 would have a 30 percent markdown if it were discounted to a special price of $0.70.)
MARKET SEGMENTATION	A marketing strategy consciously developed to produce a product or service that embodies characteristics preferred by a selected small part of a total market.
MARKET SHARE	The percentage of the total market that the firm can obtain.
MARKETING	Activities concerned with the sale and distribution of a firm's products and/or services according to needs of customers.
MARKETING CHANNEL	The pipeline through which a product flows on its way to the ultimate consumer.
MARKETING CONCEPT	The way in which a firm chooses to give special consideration to the needs, desires, and wishes of prospective and present customers.
MARKETING MIX	A blend in the proper proportions of the basic elements of product, price, promotion, and place into an integrated marketing program.

MARKETING PLAN	A plan which details the marketing activity and marketing direction a firm plans to take.
MISSION	The long-term vision of what the firm is trying to become.
NET PROFIT	The amount earned by the firm after paying operating expenses and taxes.
NET WORTH	The difference between assets and liabilities.
OBJECTIVES	Purposes, goals, and desired results for the company and its parts.
ODD PRICING	Setting the price of goods to end in an odd number (such as $9.95).
OPERATING EXPENSES	General expenses incurred by the business to generate sales.
OVERHEAD	All the costs of a business other than direct labor and materials.
OWNER'S EQUITY	The amount of cash or other assets the owner has invested in the business.
PARTNERSHIP	The joining of two or more individuals to form an organization.
PAYBACK PERIOD	The length of time required for the net revenues of an investment to equal the cost of the investment.
POLICIES	Overall guides for action and decision making to provide some consistency in company operations.
PREFERRED STOCK	A type of company financing that has characteristics of both bonds and common stock.
PRICE/ EARNINGS RATIO	The ratio of price per share to earnings per share.

PRIVATE BRAND	A brand sponsored by a merchant (e.g., Kroger) or agent as distinguished from brands sponsored by manufacturers or producers.
PRODUCT LINE	A group of products that are closely related because they satisfy a class of needs, are used together, are sold to the same customer groups, are marketed through the same type of outlet, or fall within a given price range.
PROFIT-LOSS STATEMENT	Also called the Income Statement, this financial statement lists the total sales, cost of goods sold, expenses, and taxes required in order to obtain a profit (usually for a period of a month).
PROMOTION	A blend of the three following sales activities: (1) mass, impersonal selling efforts (advertising), (2) personal sales, and (3) other activities, such as point-of-purchase displays, shows, or exhibits.
PROPRIETORSHIP	An enterprise owned by one individual. The owner and the business are one and the same and cannot be legally distinguished and separated by law.
RETAILER	A merchant or agent whose main business is to buy goods for resale to the ultimate consumer.
SAVINGS AND LOAN BANK	A bank which accepts and pays interest on deposit savings, subject to conditions prescribed by the Federal Home Loan Bank Board.
SBA	Small Business Administration. The SBA is the major governmental agency formulated to assist small businesses.
SBDC	Small Business Development Center. SBDCs are established to provide free management assistance to small business owners.

233

SERVICE BUSINESS	A firm filling non-product needs of customers. (Examples are banking and repairing firms.)
SILENT PARTNER	An investor who does not have any management responsibilities but provides capital and shares liability for any losses experienced by the entity. (Also known as a sleeping partner.)
SPAN OF CONTROL	The number of subordinates reporting to one supervisor in an organization.
SPECIALTY GOODS	Items which are bought infrequently at particular outlets after a special effort.
STRATEGY	A plan of action to attain specified objectives.
STRATEGIC PLAN	A major, comprehensive, long-term plan providing direction for a firm to accomplish its mission and objectives.
TARGET MARKET	The group of people to whom a firm directs its marketing efforts.
TRADE ASSOCIATION	An organization formed to benefit members of the same trade by informing and supporting its members.
TRADE CREDIT	Interfirm debt arising through credit sales and recorded as an account receivable by the seller and as an account payable by the buyer.
TRADEMARK	A name or logo which is given legal protection because it refers exclusively to a product. It may be used only by the trademark owner.
UNDER- CAPITALIZATION	The lack of funds necessary to optimally start and operate a venture.
UNITY OF COMMAND	The theory that an employee should have only one superior to whom he or she is directly responsible for certain matters.

VENTURE CAPITAL	Cash or cash equivalents supplied by an outside party who specializes in providing working capital for small and/or growing businesses. Venture capitalists require an equity interest in the firm in return for supplying capital assistance.
WHOLESALER	A business unit which buys and resells merchandise to retailers and other merchants and/or to industrial, institutional, and commercial users but which does not sell in significant amounts to ultimate consumers.
WORKING CAPITAL	Current assets less current liabilities.

"By determination and perseverance,

the tortoise won the race."

M.G.L.J.

CHAPTER XVII

BUSINESS RESOURCES

Think Like A Leader!!!

Look into the future with vision.

Empower others to help you accomplish the vision.

Actuate and motivate your employees for success.

Determine all the information needed to put your plan into motion.

Execute your plan.

Review your business progress continually.

M.G.L.J.

CRAFT RESOURCES

Associations

The American Ceramic Society

P.O.B. 6136
Westerville, Ohio 43086-6136
Phone: (614) 890-4700
www.ceramics.org
Publication: Ceramics Monthly

American Craft Council (ACC)

72 Spring St.
New York, NY 10012
Phone: (212) 274-0630
www.craftcouncil.org
Publication: American Craft (bi-monthly)

American Needlepoint Guild, Inc.

P.O.B. 1027
Cordova, TN 38088-1027
Phone: (901) 755-3728
www.needlepoint.org

American Quilt Study Group (AQSG)

35th & Holdrege, East Campus Loop
P.O. Box 4737
Lincoln, NE 68504-0737
Phone: (402) 472-5361
Fax: (402) 472-5428
http://www.h-net.org/~aqsg/
www.quilt.com

Art Alliance for Contemporary Glass

P.O.B. 7022
Evanston, IL 60201
Phone: (847) 869-2018
www.contempglass.org

Art Glass Association

PO Box 2537
Zanesville, OH 43702-2537
Phone: (740) 454-1194 • Toll Free: (866) 301-2421
Fax: (740) 454-1194
http://www.artglassassociation.com

Association of Crafts and Creative Industries (ACCI)

1100-H Brandywine Blvd
PO Box 3388
Zanesville, OH USA 43702-3388
Phone: (740) 452-4541
Fax: (740) 452-2552
www.accicrafts.org

Association of Crafts and Creative Industries (ACCI)

1100-H Brandywine Blvd
PO Box 3388
Zanesville, OH USA 43702-3388
Phone: (740) 452-4541
Fax: (740) 452-2552
www.accicrafts.org

Craft Organization Development Association (CODA)

Formerly the Craft Organization Directors Association

Box 7553
Asheville, NC 28802
HandMade in America
Phone: (828) 252-0121
www.codacraft.org

Craft Retailers Association for Tomorrow(CRAFT)

1900 Arch Street
Philadelphia, PA 19103
Phone:(215) 564-3484
Fax: (215) 564-2175
www.craftonline.org

Craft Yarn Council of America

P.O. Box 9
Gastonia, NC 28053
Phone: (704) 824-7838
Fax: (704) 824-0630
 Web sites addresses:
www.knitandcrochet.com
www.learntoknit.com
www.learntocrochet.com
www.warmupamerica.com
www.craftyarncouncil.com

Crochet Guild of America

PO Box 3388
Zanesville, OH 43702-3388
Phone: (740) 452-4541
Phone: (877) 852-9190 (toll free for crochet assistance)
www.crochet.org

Embroiders' Guild of America, Inc.

335 Broadway, Suite 100
Louisville, KY 40202
Phone: (502) 589-6956
www.egausa.org

| Hobby Industry Association | 319 East 54th Street |
| | Elmwood Park, New Jersey 07407 |

Hobby Industry Association 319 East 54th Street
Elmwood Park, New Jersey 07407
Phone (201) 794-1133
Fax (201) 797-0657
www.hobby.org

National Craft Association 2012 Ridge Road East #120
Rochester, NY 14622-2434
Phone: (585) 266-5472
Fax: (585) 785-3231
http://www.craftassoc.com/contact-nca.html

The Society of Arts & Crafts 175 Newbury Street
Boston, MA 02116
Phone: (617 266-1810
Fax: (617) 266-5654
www.societyofcrafts.org

Craft Publications

American Craft Magazine
American Craft Council
72 Spring St.
New York, NY 10012
Phone: (212) 274-0630
www.craftcouncil.org

Ceramics Monthly
P.O.B. 6136
Westerville, Oh 43086-6136
Phone: (614) 794-5890
Fax: (614) 891-8960
www.ceramicsmonthly.org

Crafts Beautiful Magazine
Online Magazine
www.crafts-beautiful.com

Crafts'n Things
c/o Clapper Communications Companies
2400 Devon, Suite 375, Des Plaines, IL 60018-4618
Phone: (847) 635-5800 · Fax: (847) 635-6311
www.craftsnthings.com

Crafts Magazine
P.O.B. 56015
Boulder, CO 80322
1-800-727-2387
Available through magazine subscription websites

Crafts & Sewing
100 Park Avenue
New York, NY 10017
Available through magazine subscription websites

Craftswoman
P.O. Box 848
Libertyville, IL 60048-0848
Available through magazine subscription websites

The Crafts Report
700 Orange Street
Wilmington, DE 19801
Phone: (302) 656-2209
Available through magazine subscription websites

Craftsworks for the Home
P.O. Box 413
Mount Morris, IL 61054
Available through magazine subscription websites

Craft Show Digest
P.O. Box 3275
Falls Church, VA 22043
Available through magazine subscription websites

Popular Woodworking
4700 E. Galbraith Rd.
Cincinnati, OH 45236
Phone: (877) 860-9140
www.popularwoodworking.com

Quality Crafts Market
15 W. 44th Street
New York, NY 10017
Phone: (212) 575-0140
Available through magazine subscription websites

Sunshine Artist Magazine
3210 Dade Ave.
Orlando, FL 32804
Phone: (407) 228-9772
FAX: (407) 228-9862
www.sunshineartist.com

The Wire Artist Jeweller Magazine.
Published by:
The Wire Artists Group.
PO Box 21105,
Stratford, Ontario
N5A 7V4, Canada
Phone: (519) 461-1902
Fax: (519) 461-9007
http://www.wag.on.ca/index.html

Craft Web sites of Interest

The Arts and Crafts Society
www.arts-crafts.com

Craft Magazine Subscriptions
www.heartvalues.com/craftmagazinesubscriptions.html

Craft Magazine Subscriptions
http://hopcott.com/magazines/craft.html

Craftersnet.com
www.craftersnet.com

Professional Crafters.com
www.professionalcrafters.com

ART RESOURCES

Associations/Foundations

American Society of Portrait Artists

(ASOPA)
P. O. Box 230216
Montgomery, AL 36106
info@asopa.com
Phone: 1-800-62-ASOPA
http://www.asopa.com/

American Watercolor Society

47 Fifth Avenue
New York, NY 10003
http://www.watercolor-online.com/AWS/

National Association of Artists' Organizations

1718 M Street NW, PMB #239
Washington, D.C. 20036
Phone: 202-347-6350
Fax: 202-319-1107
E-mail: naao2@naao.org.
http://www.artswire.org/Artswire/naao/

National Association of Fine Artists

PO Box 1360
Nevada City, CA 95959
Phone: (530) 470-0862
Fax: (530) 470-0256.
E-mail:info@artmarketing.com
http://artmarketing.com/

National Association of Independent Artists

www.naia-artists.org

New York Foundation for the Arts

155 Avenue of the Americas, 14th Floor
New York, NY 10013-1507
Phone: (212) 366.6900
Fax: (212) 366.1778
Email: NYFAweb@nyfa.org
http://www.nyfa.org

Art Publications

American Art Review
P.O. Box 480500
Kansas City, MO 64148
Phone: (913) 451-8801
http://www.amartrev.com/

American Art Journal
Published by Kennedy Galleries
730 Fifth Avenue
New York, NY 10019-4105
Phone: (212) 541-9600
Fax: (212) 977-3833

American Artist Magazine
770 Broadway
New York, NY 10003
Phone: (646) 654-5506
http://www.myamericanartist.com

American Arts
Published by American Council for the Arts
570 Seventh Avenue
New York, NY 10018
Available through magazine subscription websites

Art Index (an author and subject index to domestic and foreign art periodicals)
H. W. WILSON CO.
950 University Avenue
Bronx, NY 10452
http://www.artindex.com

Art Magazine
234 Eglinton Avenue, E., Suite 408
Toronto, Ont M4P1K5 Canada
Available through magazine subscription Web sites

The Artist's Magazine
P.O. Box 420235
Palm Coast, FL 32142-0235.
Phone: 800) 333-0444 or (368) 246-3370.
http://www.artistsmagazine.com/

Arts Magazine
Published by Art Digest, Inc.
23 E. 26th Street
New York, NY 10010
Available through magazine subscription Web sites

Arts Magazine
Published by Art Digest, Inc.
23 E. 26th Street
New York, NY 10010
Available through magazine subscription Web sites

Art News
122 E. 42nd Street
New York, NY 10017
Available through magazine subscription Web sites

Art Web sites of Interest

Alliance of Artists' Communities
http://www.artistcommunities.org/

American Arts Alliance
http://www.americanartsalliance.org

Americans for the Arts
http://www.artsusa.org

Art Magazine Subscriptions
www.magazines.com

The Artist Help Network
http://www.artisthelpnetwork.com

Artists in Stained Glass (AISG)
http://www.aisg.on.ca/

ArtBusiness.com
http://www.artbusiness.com

Artquotes.net
http://www.artquotes.net/directory/1artbusiness.htm

ArtsEdge
http://artsedge.kennedy-center.org

Arts Education Partnership
http://aep-arts.org

Arts Midwest
http://www.artsmidwest.org

Artworks News
http://www.urbanartworks.org/newsletter3.htm

Glass Artists.org
www.glassartists.org

MAQS - Museum of the American Quilter's Society
http://www.quiltmuseum.org

Mid-America Arts Alliance
http://www.maaa.org

Mid-Atlantic Arts Foundation
http://www.midatlanticarts.org

National Association of Fine Artists
http://www.nafa.com/

National Association of Independent Artists
www.naia-artists.org

National Endowment for the Arts
http://arts.endow.gov

National Endowment for the Humanities
http://www.neh.fed.us/

www.Sculptor.Org
309 N. Virginia Avenue
Falls Church, VA 22046

Southern Arts Federation
http://www.southarts.org

Watercolor Online
www.watercolor-online.com

Western States Arts Federation
http://www.westaf.org

World of Watercolor
http://www.worldofwatercolor.com/artassoc.htm

SELECTED NATIONAL BUSINESS ASSOCIATIONS

AMERICAN ASSOCIATION OF AFRICAN-AMERICAN WOMEN BUSINESS OWNERS
3363 Alden Place, NE,
Washington, DC 20019
Phone and Fax: (202) 399.3645
www.blackpgs.com/aawboa.

AMERICAN BUSINESS WOMEN'S ASSOCIATION (ABWA)
P. O. BOX 8728
9100 WARD PARKWAY
KANSAS CITY, MO 64114-0728
Phone 1-800-228-0007
Fax (816) 361-4991
www.abwa.org

NATIONAL ASSOCIATION FOR THE SELF EMPLOYED (NASE)
P.O.B. 612067
DFW AIRPORT
DALLAS, TX 75261-2067
PHONE: 1-800-232-6273
WWW.NASE.ORG

NATIONAL ASSOCIATION OF WOMEN BUSINESS OWNERS (NAWBO)
1100 WAYNE AVENUE STE. 830
SILVER SPRING, MD 20910
PHONE: 1-800-55-NAWBO
FAX: (703) 506-3266
WWW.NAWBO.ORG

Web sites for General Business Information

Let your creative mind envision the beautiful ocean waves, 90 degrees, sunny and a light breeze. Hold that thought for a moment and breathe. Okay, now let's get back to our real vision for fulfilling our business dreams. Spend time surfing the following information-packed Web sites. Your surfing trip may not be quite as much fun as a day at the beach, but it will certainly reap tangible benefits.

www.Inc.com

Provides information, products and online tools for entrepreneurs

www.Entreworld.org

The entrepreneurial information Web site of the Kauffman Foundation. Provides valuable entrepreneurship information.

www.NFIBonline.com

The Web site of the National Federation of Independent Business, features small business information and national and state issues facing entrepreneurs.

www.NASE.org

The National Association for the Self Employed's Web site, presents information and issues pertaining to the self employed business person.

www.USAHomeBusiness.com

The Web site of the National Association of Home Based Businesses, features resources and information.

BOOKS

Adams, Rob (2002). <u>A Good Kick in the Ass</u>. New York: Crown Business.

Alarid, William and Berle, Gustav (1997). <u>Free Help From Uncle Sam to Start Your Own Business (Or Expand the One You Have), 4th ed</u>. Santa Maria, CA: Puma Pub. Company.

Applegate, Jane (1998). <u>201 Great Ideas For Your Small Business</u>. New York: Bloomberg Press.

Bean, Roger and Radford, Russell (2000). <u>Powerful Products: Strategic Management of Successful New Product Development</u>. New York: AMACOM

Berry, Tim (1998). <u>Hurdle: The Book on Business</u>. Eugene, OR: Palo Alto Software, Inc.

Birkeland, Peter M (2002). <u>Franchising Dreams: the Lure of Entrepreneurship in America</u>. Chicago: University of Chicago Press.

Birkinshaw, Julian (2000). <u>Entrepreneurship in the Global Firm</u>. Thousand Oaks, CA: SAGE Publication.

Birley, Sue (1998). <u>Entrepreneurship</u>. Brookfield, VT: Ashgate.

Boston, Thomas D. and Century Foundation (1999). <u>Affirmative Action and Black Entrepreneurship</u>. New York: Routledge.

Butler, John (2001). <u>E-Commerce and Entrepreneurship</u>. Greenwich, CT: Information Age Publishers.

Burgess, Stephen (2002). <u>Managing Information Technology in Small Business: Challenges and Solutions</u>. Hershey, PA: Idea Group Publication.

Canefield, Jack, Hansen, Mark Victor, and Hewitt, Les (2000). <u>The Power of Focus: How to Hit Your Business, Personal and Financial Targets with Absolute Certainty</u>. Deerfield Beach, FL: Health Communications, Inc.

Carey, Charles W. (2002). <u>American Inventors, Entrepreneurs, and Business Visionaries</u>. New York: Facts on File.

Cartwright, Roger and NetLibrary, Inc. (2002). <u>The Entrepreneurial Individual</u>. Oxford, UK: Capstone Pub.

Cheney, Karen and Alderman, Lesley (1997). <u>How to Start a Successful Home Business</u>. New York: Warner Books.

Cleaver, Joanne Y. (1999). <u>Find & Keep Customers for Your Small Business</u>. Chicago: CCH Incorp.

Coulter, Mary (2001). <u>Entrepreneurship in Action</u>. Upper Saddle River, NJ: Prentice Hall.

Crainer, Stuart (2000). <u>Generation Entrepreneur: Shape Today's Business Reality, Create Tomorrow's Wealth, Do Your Own Thing</u>. London: Financial Times Prentice Hall.

Da Costa, Eduardo (2001). <u>Global E-Commerce Strategies for Small Business</u>. Cambridge, MA: MIT Press.

Debelak, Don (2001). <u>Think Big: Nine Ways to Make Millions from Your Ideas</u>. Irvine, CA: Entrepreneur Press.

Dees, J. Gregory, Emerson, Jed and Economy, Peter (2002). <u>Strategic Tools for Social Entrepreneurs: Enhancing the Performance of Your Enterprising Nonprofit</u>. Somerset, NJ: John Wiley and Sons, Inc.

DeLuca, Fred and Hayes, John Phillip (2000). <u>Start Small, Finish Big: Fifteen Key Lessons To Start –and Run—Your Own Successful Business</u>. New York: Warner Books.

Fick, David S. (2002). <u>Entrepreneurship in Africa, A Study of Success</u>. Westport, CT: Quorum Books.

Foley, James F (1999). <u>The Global Entrepreneur: Taking Your Business International</u>. Chicago: Dearborn.

Gerber, Michael E. (1995). <u>The E-Myth Revisited: Why Most Small Business Don't Work and What to Do About It</u>. New York: Harper Collins Publishers.

Goltz, Jay with Oesterricher, Judy (1998). <u>The Street-Smart Entrepreneur: 133 Tough Lessons I Learned the Hard Way</u>. Omaha, NB: Addicus Books.

Gravely, Melvin J (1995). <u>The Black Entrepreneur's Guide to Success</u>. Edgewood, MD: Duncan & Duncan.

Gravely, Melvin J., II (1997). <u>Making It Your Business: The Personal Transition from Employee to Entrepreneur</u>. Cincinnati: Impact Group Consultants.

Hall, Doug (2001). <u>Jump Start Your Business Brain</u>. Cincinnati: Brain Brew Books.

Hayes, Cassandra (2002). <u>Black Enterprise Guide to Building Your Career</u>. New York: John Wiley.

Hisrich, Robert D and Peters, Michael P. (1995). <u>Entrepreneurship: Starting, Developing, and Managing A New Enterprise 3rd ed</u>. Chicago: Irwin.

Hitt, Michael A. (2002). <u>Strategic Entrepreneurship: Creating A New Integrated Mindset</u>. Malden, MA: Blackwell.

Inman, Katherine (2000). <u>Women's Resources in Business Start-up: A Study of Black and White Women Entrepreneurs</u>. New York: Garland Publisher.

Janal, Daniel S. (1997). <u>101 Successful Businesses You Can Start on the Internet</u>. New York: Van Nostrand Reinhold.

Johnson, Van R. (2000). <u>Entrepreneurial Management and Public Policy</u>. Huntington, NY: Nova Science Publishers.

Kijakazi, Kilolo (1997). <u>African-American Economic Development and Small Business Ownership</u>. New York: Garland Pub.

Kotter, John P. and Cohen, Dan S. (2002). <u>The Heart of Change: Real-Life Stories of How People Change Their Organizations</u>. Watertown, MA: Harvard Business School Press.

Krass, Peter (1999). <u>The Book of Entrepreneur's Wisdom, Classic Writings by Legendary Entrepreneurs</u>. Somerset, NJ: John Wiley & Sons.

Kuratko, Donald F. and Hodgetts, Richard M. (2000). <u>Entrepreneurship: A Contemporary Approach</u>. Fort Worth, TX: Dryden Press.

Lacy, Harold R. (1998). <u>Financing Your Business Dreams with Other People's Money: How and Where to Find Money for Start-up and Growing Businesses</u>. Traverse City, MI: Sage Creek Press.

Lane, Marc J. (2001). <u>Advising Entrepreneurs: Dynamic Strategies For Financial Growth</u>. New York: Wiley.

Lipman, Frederick D. (1998). <u>Financing Your Business with Venture Capital: Strategies to Grow Your Enterprise with Outside Investors</u>. Rocklin, CA: Prima.

Lodish, Leonard, Morgan, Howard Lee, and Kallianpur, Amy (2001). Entrepreneurial Marketing: Lessons from Wharton's Pioneering MBA Course. New York: Wiley.

McDaniel, Bruce (2002). Entrepreneurship and Innovation: An Economic Approach. Armonk, NY: M.E. Sharpe.

Meyers, G. Dale and Heppard, Kurt A. (2000). Entrepreneurship As Strategy: Competing on the Entrepreneurial Edge. Thousand Oaks, CA: SAGE Publications, Inc.

Moore, Dorothy P. and Buttner, E. Holly (1997). Women Entrepreneurs: Moving Beyond The Glass Ceiling. Thousand Oaks, CA: SAGE Publications.

Murtha, Thomas P., Lenway, Stephanie Ann, and Hart, Jeffrey A. (2003). Managing New Industry Creation: Global Knowledge Formation and Entrepreneurship in High Technology. Palo Alto, CA: Stanford University Press.

Oden, Howard W. (1997). Managing Corporate Culture, Innovation, and Entrepreneurship. Westport, CT.: Quorum Books.

Ryan, Rob (2001). Smartups. New York: Cornell University Press.

Sexton, Donald L (1999). The Blackwell Handbook of Entrepreneurship. Malden, MA: Blackwell Business.

Sharma, Poonam (1999). The Harvard Entrepreneur's Club Guide to Starting Your Own Business. New York: John Wiley.

Stephenson, James (2001). Entrepreneur's Ultimate Start-up Directory. Irvine, CA: Entrepreneur Press.

Stolze, William (1996). Start Up: An Entrepreneur's Guide to Launching and Managing a New Business. Hawthorne, NJ: Career Press.

Sullivan, Robert (1998). The Small Business Start-Up Guide. Great Falls, VA: Information International.

Sullivan, William R. (1997). Entrepreneur Magazine: Human Resources for Small Business. New York: John Wiley.

Sutton, Garrett et al (2001). Own Your Own Corporation: Why the Rich Own Their Own Companies and Everyone Else Works For Them. New York: Warner Books.

Tabrrok, Alexander (2002). <u>Entrepreneurial Economics: Bright Ideas from the Dismal Science</u>. New York: Oxford University Press.

Turner, Colin (2002). <u>Lead to Succeed: Creating Entrepreneurial Organizations</u>. New York, London: Texere.

Wallace, Robert L (2000). <u>Soul Food: 52 Principles of Black Entrepreneurial Success</u>. Cambridge, MA: Perseus Pub.

Williams, Bernadette (2002). <u>Black Enterprise Guide to Technology for Entrepreneurs</u>. New York: Wiley.

Williams, Edward E. and Thompson, James R. (1998). <u>Entrepreneurship and Productivity</u>. Lanham, MD: University Press of America.

Woodard, Michael D (1997). <u>Black Entrepreneurs in America: Stories of Struggle and Success</u>. New Brunswick, NJ: Rutgers University Press.

Young, Ruth C, Francis, Joe D, and Young, Christopher H. (1999). <u>Entrepreneurship, Private and Public</u>. Lanham, MD: University Press of America.

INDEXES

<u>Business Periodicals Index</u>. New York: Wilson.
Subject index to articles in the fields of accounting, advertising, public relations, banking, economics, finance and investments, insurance, labor, management, marketing, and taxation. Also includes information on specific businesses, industries, and trades.

<u>Readers' Guide to Periodical Literature</u>. New York: Wilson.
Author and subject index to the contents of over 150 general and nontechnical magazines. A good starting point for finding information on a wide variety of topics.

<u>Social Sciences and Humanities Index</u>. Vols. 1-27, 1916-1974, formerly called <u>International Index</u>. Author and subject index to periodicals in the fields of anthropology, economics, environmental science, geography, law and criminology, political science, psychology public administration, and sociology.

DICTIONARIES AND ENCYCLOPEDIAS

Middle Market Directory. New York: Dun and Bradstreet. Annual. This directory provides information about companies whose net worth ranges from $500,000 to $900,000, including utilities, transportation companies, banks and trust companies, stockbrokers, mutual and stock insurance companies, wholesalers, and retailers. The companies are listed alphabetically, geographically, and by product classification (S.I.C., Standard Industrial Classification).

Million Dollar Directory. New York: Dun and Bradstreet. Annual. Arranged as is Middle Market Directory. This compilation provides information about companies with a net worth of $1 million or more. It also contains a management directory that lists officers and directors and their affiliations.

Poor's Register of Corporations, Directors and Executives, United States and Canada. New York: Standard and Poor's Corporation. Annual. Volume I contains alphabetical listing of corporations with directors and executives. Volume 2 is a register of directors and executives of the companies listed in Volume 1. Volume 3 contains Standard Industrial Classification and geographical indexes. Supplements are issued in April, July, and October.

List of Small Business Investment Companies. Washington: U.S. Government Printing Office. Irregular.

National Minority Business Directory. Minneapolis: National Minority Business Directories. Annual. This specialized directory lists over 7,000 minority firms (50 percent or more owned by minority group members), classified by product. A cross-reference index aids in finding the appropriate classification. Computer disks are also available. Published by TRY US Resources, Inc. (612) 781-6819.

Thomas Register of American Manufacturers. New York: Thomas Publishing Company. Annual. Manufacturers are arranged according to product, and the manufacturers of each product are listed geographically. Alphabetical indexes to manufacturers, trade names, and specific products facilitate its use.

SPECIAL LISTS

Black Enterprise. New York, Monthly. The "top-100" black-owned businesses that gross more than $1 million annually are listed in the June issue each year.

Forbes. New York. Semi-monthly. The "Annual Report on American Industry" is in the first issue each year. It lists companies according to profitability, growth and pure stock gain over a five-year period. The "Annual Directory Issue" (May 15) ranks the top 500 corporations in sales, stock market value, assets, and profits.

Fortune. New York. Semi-monthly. "The Directory of Largest Corporations" is an annual feature in several parts. The May issue lists the 500 largest U.S. industrial companies by sales. The June issue lists the second-largest 500 U.S. industrial companies. The July issue lists the largest nonindustrial corporations and the fifty largest companies in banking, life insurance, diversified financial services, retailing, transportation, and utilities. The August issue lists the largest corporations outside the United States, and the September issue lists the 300 largest corporations outside the United States, and the September issue lists the 300 largest banks outside the country.

Encyclopedia of Associations. Detroit: Gale Research. Revised approximately every two years. This classified directory lists over 12,000 organized groups. It lists for each, the address, phone number, chief official, a description, publications, and other pertinent information. The alphabetical and key-word index is helpful in locating an association if one does not know its exact name. Supplementary lists of new associations are issued quarterly.

The Foundation Directory. New York: Compiled by the Foundation Center and distributed by Columbia University Press. This directory lists foundations by state. Each entry includes the corporate names, address, purpose, activities, and pertinent financial data.

ATLASES AND MAPS

Ginsburg, Norton. Atlas of Economic Development. Chicago: University of Chicago Press. This atlas offers graphic representations of data on population, land resources, transportation, energy generation and consumption. Each map is accompanied by textual material explaining and summarizing the analyzed data.

Rand McNally Commercial Atlas and Marketing Guide. New York: Rand McNally, Annual. Limited to U.S. marketing data, this atlas provides summaries and analyses of statistics by state in the areas of agriculture, manufacturing, population, retail trade, and transportation.

BIBLIOGRAPHIES AND GUIDES

Coman, Edwin T. Sources of Business Information. rev. ed. Berkeley and Los Angeles: University of California Press. . The first four chapters of this guide deal with methodology and the range of business sources. The remaining chapters treat such specific fields as accounting, real estate and insurance, and management. Limited to American and Canadian sources, and a few from England.

Encyclopedia of Business Information Sources. 2 vols. Detroit: Gale. Volume I is organized alphabetically by topic, with sub headings by type of source. Lists primary and secondary sources of information.

PERIODICALS

Academy of Management Journal. Tampa, FL., Quarterly.

Accounting Review. Sarasota, Fl.: American Accounting Association. Quarterly.

Administrative Science Quarterly. Ithaca, NY: Cornell University Graduate School of Business and Public Administration. Quarterly.

Black Enterprise. New York. Monthly.

Business Week. New York: McGraw-Hill. Weekly.

Commerce America. Washington: U.S. Department of Commerce. Bi-weekly. Order from U.S. Government Printing Office.

Dun's Review. New York: Dun & Bradstreet. Monthly.

Federal Reserve Bulletin. Washington: U.S. Board of Governors of the Federal Reserve System. Monthly.

Forbes. New York. Semimonthly.

Fortune. New York, Semimonthly.

Harvard Business Review. Boston: Harvard University Graduate School of Business Administration. Monthly.

Industry Week. Cleveland, OH: Penton Publishing Company. Weekly.

Money. Chicago. Monthly.

Monthly Labor Review. Washington: U.S. Government Printing Office. Monthly

Nation's Business. Washington: Chamber of Commerce of the United States. Monthly.

Survey of Current Business. Washington: U.S. Department of Commerce. Order from U.S. Government Printing Office. Monthly. Supplemented weekly by Business Statistics.

Wall Street Journal. New York: Dow Jones. 5 issues per week.

ADDITIONAL GENERAL REFERENCES

http://www.census.gov/epcd/mwb97/us/us.html#Black - Census Bureau information for minority and women-owned businesses

http://www.census.gov/prod/ec97/e97cs-2.pdf - census information

http://www.census.gov/Press-Release/www/2001/cb01-61.html - women-owned businesses, numbers from 1997

http://www.nfwbo.org/minority/AllMinority.pdf - minority women business owners data

http://www.census.gov/epcd/mwb97/us/us.html#Black - Census Bureau info for minority and women-owned businesses

http://www.nfwbo.org/minority/AllMinority.pdf - Minority women business owners data

ANNUAL STATEMENT STUDIES　　　　　The Risk Management Association (Formerly Robert Morris Associates)
One Liberty Place
1650 Market Street, Suite 2300
Philadelphia, PA 19103
Phone: 1-800-677-7621; (215) 446-4000
Fax: (215) 446-4101
www.rmahq.org

KEY BUSINESS RATIOS

The D&B Corporation
103 JFK Parkway
Short Hills, NJ 07078
Phone:1- 800-234-3867
For International Inquiries – 1-800-932-0025
www.dnb.com

"There is no success unless you have successors."

M.G.L.J.

APPENDIX

SAMPLE BUSINESS FORMS

"For all the trials and tears of time,

for every hill I have to climb,

my heart sings but a grateful song—

these are the things that make me strong."

Anonymous

SAMPLE PURCHASE ORDER FORM

PURCHASE ORDER

Date:_____   P.O. # _____

(assign in sequence)

TO: (NAME OF SUPPLIER)

How to Ship: (UPS or other)
Terms: (will pay when billed, etc.)

Deliver By: (date needed)

BILL TO: (NAME AND ADDRESS OF FIRM TO RECEIVE BILL)

Shipping & Packing Instructions:

SHIP TO: (NAME AND ADDRESS OF WHERE GOODS SHOULD BE SENT)

Quantity	Item #	Description	Unit Cost	Discount	Total

GRAND TOTAL

Ordered by:_____

NOTE Please show our order # on all shipments or correspondence, and advise if unable to meet required delivery date.

ANY CHANGES IN THIS PURCHASE ORDER MUST BE IN WRITING

Any such failure that results in documentable third party costs will be deducted from the vendor's invoice. Failure on the part of vendor to meet terms and delivery dates will void this Purchase Order unless such charges are authorized in revised Purchase Order.

BILLING STATEMENT

FIRM NAME, ADDRESS AND CONTACT NUMBERS

Statement Date:_____   **Acct.**
No.:_____

TO: CUSTOMER NAME

Date	Terms	Items or Services Purchased	Amount	Remarks

Please Pay This Amount: _____

Current	30 days	60 days	90 days and over

*Note: Terms Net _____ Days

PETTY CASH RECORD

DATE	PAID TO	FOR	APPROVED BY	BALANCE ON HAND

BALANCE SHEET

ASSETS

	Present Year	**Prior Year**

Current Assets
   Cash (in hand, in banks)
   Accounts receivable (subtract
    allowance for bad debts)
   Inventories
   Prepayments
   Investments (at cost)
   Other _____

Total current assets:

Fixed Assets
   Land
   Buildings
   Machinery
   Office Equipment
   Other _____
    Subtotal
   Less accumulated depreciation
Net fixed assets:
Other assets and deferred charges
Intangibles (goodwill, patents, trademarks)

Total assets

LIABILITIES

Current Liabilities:
   Accounts payable
   Notes payable
   Accrued expenses payable
   Federal and state income taxes payable
   Other _____
Total current liabilities

Long Term Liabilities
   Interest (notes payable after one year)
   Other _____
Total liabilities:

INCOME STATEMENT

	Present Year	Prior Year
Revenues:		
Net Sales (operating revenues, less discounts)	_____	_____
Other income:	_____	_____
Total revenue:	_____	_____
Cost of Sales:		
Inventory	_____	_____
Royalties	_____	_____
Other _____	_____	_____
Total cost of sales:	_____	_____
Gross profit or loss:	_____	_____
Operating Expenses		
Selling Expense (Adv., payroll, travel, entertainment, etc.)	_____	_____
General Administration (Heat, light, rent, etc.)	_____	_____
Other _____	_____	_____
Net income before taxes:	_____	_____
Income taxes:	_____	_____
Net Profit:	_____	_____

"Your reputation is your most valuable asset."

M.G.L.J.

NOTES

[1] http://www.womensbusinessresearch.org/Research/5-6-2003/5-6-2003.htm

[2] http://www.craftsreport.com/industrystats/industrystats.html

[3] Petzak, Mary E., The Internet: Is It Making A Difference in Sales of Craft Works? The Crafts Report, http://www.craftsreport.com/current_issue/feature.html

[4] The $14 Billion Crafts Industry: The Cody Survey Results Prove that Crafts are BIG Business. The Crafts Report, May 2001.

[5] Kenneth Lawyer and Clifford Baumback, How to Organize and Operate a Small Business, 6th Edition (Englewood Cliffs, New Jersey: Prentiuce Hall, 1979, p.56.

[6] Hal B. Pickel, "Personality and Success: An evaluation of Personal Characteristics of Successful Small Business Managers," Small Business Research Series No. 4. Small Business Administration (Washington, DC: G.P.O.), 1964.

[7] Small Business Administration, "Keys to Business Success," Office of Management Assistance (1973), p. 37.

[8] James F. DeCarlo and Paul Lyons, " A Comparison of Selected Personal Characteristics of Minority and Non-Minority Female Entrepreneurs," Journal of Small Business Management, 17 October 1979, pp.25-26.

[9] Ibid, p. 25

[10] Ibid

[11] William Glueck, "Entrepreneurial and Family Firms," Management (Hinsdale, Illinois: Dryden Press, 1977), p. 57.

[12] Ibid, p. 50

[13] Ralph Stogdill, Handbook of Leadership (New York: The Free Press, 1974), pp. 76-82.

[14] Ibid, p. 167

[15] Charles B. Swayne and William R. Tucker, The Effective Entrepreneur (Morristown, NJ: General Learning Press, 1973), p. 35.

[16] I*bid., p. 35*

[17] Keith Davis, <u>Human Behavior at Work</u> (New York: McGraw Hill, Inc., 1977) p. 26.

[18] Kenneth R. Van Voorhis, <u>Entrepreneurship and Small Business Management</u> (Boston: Allyn & Bacon, 1980), p. 29.

A BUSINESS OF YOUR OWN
Business Publications and Services for the Entrepreneurial Woman

"Our purpose is to assist the entrepreneurial woman in pulling together the intricate components necessary to make a small business a success!!!"

FACT SHEET

A BUSINESS OF YOUR OWN is a multifaceted service firm that specializes in business publications and services designed to assist women in starting and managing small businesses.

A BUSINESS OF YOUR OWN publishes information that inspire, motivate, educate and help the female entrepreneur grow and develop skills to manage a successful business. Our publications range from basic startup manuals to detailed guide books for implementing and managing a specific business.

A BUSINESS OF YOUR OWN does more than just present the nuts and bolts of initiating a business between the covers of a manual. We are different because entrepreneurial women are different! We also offer strategy sessions, workshops, seminars, business development retreats, and much more...

ABOUT OUR COMPREHENSIVE START UP MANUALS.......

The informational publications from *A BUSINESS OF YOUR OWN* reflect an enormous amount of in-depth research and the expertise of many noted professionals. Our comprehensive business start-up publications utilize a uniquely designed step-by-step, hands-on approach to business formulation. Crucial business development and management information is provided in an easy to understand format followed by questions for the entrepreneur to address. The summarization of the answers to these questions will enable the entrepreneurially minded woman in pulling together the major components of their business. Worksheets are provided for the purpose of providing assistance in preparing a business plan. All business start-up publications are designed so that upon completion, the entrepreneur will have a detailed business plan for their venture.

**Our manuals are: *Currently researched   *Informational *Practical *Systematic *Motivational
*Comprehensive *Easy to understand *Designed for the Entrepreneurial Woman**

Additional Publications for the Entrepreneurial Woman

- Starting a Child Care Center $49.95 (Paperback-81/2 by 11)

- Starting a Flower and Gift Shop $49.95 (Paperback-81/2 by 11)

Shipping and Handling Costs: $4.00/manual   ▲   *Traditional Discounts Offered to the Trade.*

A BUSINESS OF YOUR OWN
P.O.B. 210662 ■ Nashville, Tennessee 37221-0662
Phone: (615) 646-3708 ■   Fax: (615) 662-8584
E-mail: Success@womaninbiz.com   Website: www.abusinessofyourown.com